T.S. Eliot's Personal Waste Land

T.S. Eliot's
Personal Waste Land

Exorcism of the Demons

James E. Miller, Jr. 1920 –

The Pennsylvania State University Press

University Park and London

Library of Congress Cataloging in Publication Data

Miller, James Edwin, 1920–
    T.S. Eliot's personal waste land.

    Includes bibliographical references and index.
    1. Eliot, Thomas Stearns, 1888–1965. The waste
land. I. Title.
PS3509.L43W373   821'.9'12   76-40424
ISBN 0-271-01237-4

Printed in the United States of America

for Barbara

> *As we grow older*
> *The world becomes stranger, the pattern more complicated*
> *Of dead and living. Not the intense moment*
> *Isolated, with no before and after,*
> *But a lifetime burning in every moment*

"East Coker"

. . . he is haunted by a demon, a demon against which he feels powerless, because in its first manifestation it has no face, no name, nothing; and the words, the poem he makes, are a kind of form of exorcism of this demon.

T.S. Eliot, "The Three Voices of Poetry"

Contents

Preface

T.S. *Eliot's Personal Waste Land* is intended as a work of literary criticism, but by its very nature it touches some sensitive areas of biography. Whenever I have dealt with biography, it has been my purpose and intention to move always from the life to the work, so that the ultimate focus of the book is on the poetry. My only interest in the life is the light it might shed on the poetry.

But any critic dealing with Eliot, bringing together aspects of biography and elements of poems, must be acutely aware of the large "no trespassing" signs that the poet himself conspicuously posted, both early and late, in his critical commentary. As early as 1917, in "Tradition and the Individual Talent," where he propounded his extraordinary "impersonal theory of poetry," Eliot wrote: "Honest criticism and sensitive appreciation are directed not upon the poet but upon the poetry."[1] And as late as 1956, in "The Frontiers of Criticism," Eliot wrote: "For myself, I can only say that a knowledge of the springs which released a poem is not necessarily a help towards understanding the poem: too much information about the origins of the poem may even break my contact with it."[2]

These and similar statements have for a long time discouraged Eliot's commentators from entering the forbidden territory of Eliot's biography[3] (although some critics like Hugh Kenner have speculated—and, I think, often fruitfully—on connections between the life and the poetry). Indeed, Eliot's critical pronouncements in a general way served as the basis for the development of the New Criticism, which in turn served as the basis for the method of reading Eliot's poems. Has any other poet of comparable stature ever been given so large a critical voice in determining how his own poems would be read and experienced?

In my zeal for connecting some aspects of biography and poetry, I realize, then, that I am flying in the face of the many strictures that Eliot issued against such connections. But I find the grounds for ignoring Eliot's warning-signs compelling. First, I believe that his criticism itself has significant biographical implications and connections, which I deal with in outline in Chapter 4. And Eliot himself has provided something of a basis for de-dogmatizing and de-mythologizing his critical pronouncements in "To Criticize the Critic" (1961), where he significantly disavowed many of his early pronouncements which had been codified into critical law by his followers.[4] Second, I believe that in exploring the "springs which released" *The Waste Land,* I am ultimately dealing not simply with the poem's origins, but in a fundamental way with its meaning. That is, I am convinced that in the case of *The Waste Land* the origins are embedded so deeply in the manuscripts, published in 1971, as well as in the published version whose existence dates from 1922, that these origins or "springs" virtually constitute poetic meaning. Thus my illumination of them leads not away from the poetry but more deeply into it—as the concentration of the major portion of the book on the successive parts of the poem demonstrates.

I can think of no better conception of the relation of biography and art than that which informs Richard Ellmann's *Golden Codgers: Biographical Speculations* (1973): "A secret or at least tacit life under-lies the one we are thought to live. We are silent about it either because we do not know it, or, knowing it, find it dull, or because, for reasons of fondness or embarrassment, we are tender on its account. One of the pleasures of writing novels and poems is that this sub-surface life can be drawn upon and transformed without incurring the responsibilities of autobiography or history, yet with happier obligations imposed by an art form" (p. ix).[5] I have at-tempted to reconstruct from available materials a part of that vital "sub-surface life" of T.S. Eliot, and to demonstrate (in following many of the signals that he himself seemed to be sending out) how that "sub-surface life" became reflected imaginatively in *The Waste Land.*

In discussing the future of biography, Ellmann says: "Biographies will continue to be archival, but the best ones will offer speculations, conjectures, hypotheses. The attempt to connect disparate elements, to describe the movements within the mind as if they were move-ments within the atom, to label the most elusive particles, will be-come more venturesome" (p. 15). What I have written is of course not a biography, but where I have been biographical I have been venturesome and used conjecture in the way, I trust, Ellmann here recommends. I am conscious that I have gone considerably beyond his own discussion of Eliot's *Waste Land* manuscripts. But, in doing so, I am fully aware of his admonition that "we cannot know completely the intricacies with which any mind negotiates with its surroundings to produce literature. The controlled seething out of which great works comes is not likely to yield all its secrets" (p. 16). My conjectures will, I trust, carry us beyond where we are in our present understanding of Eliot and *The Waste Land.* Yet there will remain a residue out of reach.

I must stress once more that my purpose has not been to examine merely how *The Waste Land* came to be, but also to explore what, at its deepest levels, it means. Often in *The Waste Land,* the meaning is discovered in the becoming; and, indeed, the becoming is discovered to be the meaning. Moreover, that meaning is not ultimately dependent on the particulars of biographical identification explored. If not these particulars, then something like them gave the poem its coherence. We may never come (or need) to know all the specifics.

In 1933 Eliot wrote: "But what a poem means is as much what it means to others as what it means to the author; and indeed, in the course of time a poet may become merely a reader in respect to his own works, forgetting his original meaning—or without forgetting, merely changing."[6] There is confession here, of sorts, that there was a meaning to *The Waste Land* that its readers did not recover. Eliot is willing to agree with his readers that the poem means what they have said it means, what he didn't realize it meant when he was writing it. But his comment tells us, too, in that last addition ("without forgetting, merely changing") that he had not forgotten his original meaning, that it was still there for him, under the meanings the readers had constructed over it. I might turn Eliot's quote around as defining in large part my purpose: "But what a poem means is as much what it means to the *author* as what it means to others." What I have attempted to do is recover that "original meaning" that Eliot insisted was there.

And I hope I need not add that I pursue that "original meaning" not to diminish Eliot or his poem, but to follow out his own various "faint clews & indirections," and to enhance his poem by coming to understand its deepest undercurrents and to feel the vibrations of its lowest—or highest—frequencies.

Acknowledgments

Students in my seminar on the American 1920s listened patiently to a first version of this book in the fall of 1974 and helped to give it shape: Russell Hahn, Carol Levenson, Gloria Maxwell, Jeffrey Rubin-Dorsky, Creath Thorne, and Richard Vine. I am much indebted, as I reveal in the text and notes, to John Peter's essays of 1952 and 1969. G. Wilson Knight's comments in the *Times Literary Supplement* of 1972 inspired me to write to him; his response, and especially his 1972 *Denver Quarterly* essay, were most helpful. I also found discussions with my University of Chicago colleague Dr. Harry Trosman, Professor in the Department of Psychiatry, both enlightening and useful. I am most grateful to those who read the manuscript and made suggestions for improvement: John M. Pickering, Audrey T. Rodgers, Marie Secor, Robert Secor, Stanley Weintraub. William Oman acted as both friend and counselor; his assistance came at exactly the right moment. A Senior Fellowship Award for 1975 from the National Endowment for the Humanities enabled me to revise and complete the manuscript.

Although all these people and many others helped in ways that cannot be easily acknowledged, only I must be held accountable for the book I have written and the ideas it contains.

1

Prologue

A Curious Shudder

I sometimes hold it half a sin
  To put in words the grief I feel;
  For words, like Nature, half reveal
And half conceal the Soul within.

Alfred, Lord Tennyson

I begin with, of all things, a poem from Alfred, Lord Tennyson's *In Memoriam,* the seventh of the sequence, in which the author describes his melancholy visit to the empty house of his now dead friend, Arthur Henry Hallam:

Dark house, by which once more I stand
  Here in the long unlovely street,
  Doors, where my heart was used to beat
So quickly, waiting for a hand,

A hand that can be clasp'd no more—
  Behold me, for I cannot sleep,
  And like a guilty thing I creep
At earliest morning to the door.

He is not here; but far away
  The noise of life begins again,
  And ghastly thro' the drizzling rain
On the bald street breaks the blank day.

Eliot quoted this Tennyson poem in his essay introducing an edition of Tennyson's poems published in 1936, and reprinted the essay in *Essays Ancient and Modern* and also in his 1950 edition of *Selected Essays.*

Not only did Eliot quote the Tennyson poem in its entirety, but he made some extravagant comments on it that we should listen to carefully—comments which I believe to be both surprising and revealing: "This is great poetry, economical of words, a universal emotion in what could only be an English town: and it gives me the shudder that I fail to get from anything in *Maud* [a poem just previously commented on by Eliot]. But such a passage, by itself, is not *In Memoriam: In Memoriam* is the whole poem. It is unique: it is a long poem made by putting together lyrics, which have only the unity and continuity of a diary, the concentrated diary of a man confessing himself. It is a diary of which we have to read every word" (p. 291).[1] There are so many things calling for commentary in this passage that it is hard to know where to begin. It might be best to begin again with the Tennyson poem, to have fresh in mind just what poem it is that elicits such extravagant response, and linger over some of the Tennysonian phrases: the speaker returns at night to the house of his dead friend, located "Here in the long *unlovely* street," where his heart "was used to beat/ So quickly, waiting for a hand. . . . " But realizing that the hand "can be clasp'd no more," the speaker seems to be filled with self-pity, mixed with a compulsion for exposure ("Behold me," he says) and a compulsion for guilt: "Behold me, for I cannot sleep,/ And like a guilty *thing* I creep/ At earliest morning to the door." The last stanza begins with a revelation that by now we might already know—"He [that is, the dead friend] is not here." And then the poem turns from the empty house, turns away from deep emotion to empty existence: "The noise of life begins again,/ And ghastly thro' the drizzling rain/ On the bald street breaks the blank day."

There are many surprises in Eliot's response to this Tennysonian lyric. As readers who have been brought up on Eliot's "impersonal theory" of poetry and trained in Eliot's theory that poetry is never simply the expression of emotion but rather an "escape from emotion" through some complicated formula like an "objective correlative"—as such sophisticated readers we might well have read this

Tennysonian lyric and shuddered at its violation of all the rules of good impersonal poetry, at its indecent personal exposure of a heart that "was used to beat/ So quickly at the approach of a friend," at its imprecision of diction in such blurred phrases as "*unlovely* street" and "guilty *thing*," at its slight absurdity in beginning with a direct address to the "Dark house" and with its delayed command to the "Dark house" to "Behold me" (an imperative that seems to supply more needed syllables than genuine meaning for the poem).

The question arises: why did this poem give T.S. Eliot "the shudder" of genuine response that he records in this essay, a shudder that causes him to say, simply, "This is great poetry, economical of words, a universal emotion . . . "? Eliot's extravagant claims for the lines seem strangely remote from the passionate intensity of his highly personal response. We might readily agree on the universality of the emotion found in grief for a dead friend, but we might begin to question the universality of the inconsolable sense of loss as it becomes mixed with guilt ("like a guilty thing I creep"), and the sense deepening to feelings of futility and meaninglessness, as the poet turns back to "the noise of life"—as on "the bald street breaks the blank day." However *great, economical,* or *universal* Tennyson's lines, the particular circumstances of his grief appear unique: he and Arthur Hallam became close friends at Cambridge, where both were undergraduates; later Hallam became engaged to Tennyson's sister; Hallam's sudden death at the age of twenty-four (in 1833) affected Tennyson profoundly, and he at once began the long elegy that was published as *In Memoriam* in 1850. Eliot's emphasis on the universality of the emotion in Tennyson's lyric suggests his own deep identification with it—and inspires wonder as to whether there is not a similar structure of circumstances in Eliot's own life.

So moved is Eliot by this lyric that he goes on to praise *In Memoriam* for its uniqueness—its quality of a "concentrated diary of a man confessing himself." Diary? Confessing? Here Eliot seems to be responding to Tennyson's poem for all the wrong reasons—wrong reasons that the younger Eliot had spelled out so carefully in "Tradition and the Individual Talent" back in 1917, his earliest essay preserved in his *Selected Essays*. The young Eliot wrote (in only one of several similar sentences arguing with Wordsworth's phrase "emotion recollected in tranquility"): "It is not in his personal emotions, the emotions provoked by particular events in his life, that the poet is in any way remarkable or interesting" (p.10). This young Eliot stands almost repudiated by the older Eliot's effusive enthusiasm for a highly personal Tennysonian lyric plucked from a "unique . . . long poem" that was "made by putting together lyrics, which have only the unity of a diary." We are confronted with a remarkable transfiguration, from a young critic who called for an "emotion which has its life in the poem and not in the history of the poet" (p. 11) to the older (or mature) critic who can work up genuine enthusiasm for a confessional diary consisting of lyrics containing emotions which have a life in both the poetry and the poet. (We should note in passing the implications here for what has come to be called in our time "confessional poetry.")

There is, I believe, a solution to the puzzle which I pose, but it is best revealed after a brief examination of Eliot's continuing comments in his Tennyson essay, comments which immediately follow those quoted above: "Apparently Tennyson's contemporaries, once they had accepted *In Memoriam*, regarded it as a message of hope and reassurance to their rather fading Christian faith. *It happens now and then that a poet by some strange accident expresses the mood of his generation, at the same time that he is expressing a mood of his own which is quite remote from that of his generation.* This is not a question of insincerity: there is an amalgam of yielding and opposition below the level of consciousness" (p. 291; italics added.) This passage, especially when placed in the context of a number of other of Eliot's comments (cited later), clearly reveals that Eliot has reference to himself and his own poem, *The Waste Land*—which over and over again was described by critics as expressing the "mood" of a generation, and which Eliot over and over again insisted was really only expressing a "mood of his own." Because Eliot seems to be talking somewhat obliquely about himself here, it is of great interest to observe how *he* read Tennyson's *In Memoriam*—for hints from him as to how *we* might read *The Waste Land*.

Eliot felt free with *In Memoriam* (as we shall feel free later with *The Waste Land*) to explore Tennyson's meanings on two levels, the conscious level and "below the level of consciousness." He wrote: "Tennyson himself, on the conscious level of the man who talks to reporters and poses for photographers, to judge from remarks made

in conversation and recorded in his son's memoir, consistently asserted a convinced, if somewhat sketchy, Christian belief. . . . Nevertheless, I get a very different impression from *In Memoriam* from
that which Tennyson's contemporaries seem to have got. It is of a
very much more interesting and tragic Tennyson." Eliot goes on to
stress that, although Tennyson repeatedly expressed, on the conscious level, the faith of a believer, on the unconscious level he
expressed something else: "Tennyson is distressed by the idea of a
mechanical universe; he is naturally, in lamenting his friend, teased
by the hope of immortality and reunion beyond death. Yet the renewal craved for seems at best but a continuance, or a substitute for
the joys of friendship upon earth" (p. 292).

It does not require, I believe, a very bold imagination to perceive
that in talking about Tennyson, Eliot is talking indirectly about himself; indeed, it is almost as if he is inviting some future critic to deal
with him and *The Waste Land* as he has dealt with *In Memoriam*. In
short, he seems to be saying something like this—*The Waste Land* has
been accepted as expressing the mood of my generation, but in fact
it expresses a quite personal mood, a mood that may be detected
beneath the surface of the poem, in labyrinths of consciousness or
unconsciousness that are awaiting penetration. If this were all that
Eliot is saying, perhaps it would not be enough to justify the space
here allotted to his essay on Tennyson. But I believe that he is
revealing more—indeed, I think he is pointing to the substance of
that personal content of *The Waste Land* to be found on the lower
levels. This revelation comes, I believe, in Eliot's deeply felt response—
"shudder"—to Tennyson's slight lyric expressing his grief for his
dead friend as he approaches the dark house in the long "unlovely
street" and then, filled with "memory and desire," turns from the
empty house in the "drizzling rain" and looks on in despair as the
"blank day" breaks on the "bald street." It is significant to note the
associations in Eliot's mind as he writes his essay on Tennyson: he
moves almost immediately from the lyric expressing intense grief for
the loss of a dead friend to memory of his own *The Waste Land*—
another poem that, on the lower levels, grieves the loss of a dead
friend, but which, like *In Memoriam*, has been read primarily as a
public poem expressing the mood of a generation: in both poems,
the view of the world has been generated by the highly personalized

state of consciousness—the sense of loss—of the "speaker" (or "meditator"), and not, as so often affirmed, the other way around. I want to explore those lower levels, but next I must present some biographical data, first on myself, and then on Eliot.

2

An Interpretation
Suppressed

Amazement and Disgust

I often say to myself about Calamus—perhaps it means more or less than I thought myself—means different: perhaps I don't know what it all means—perhaps never did know.

Walt Whitman

Only a few short years ago (10 November 1968) we learned the startling news in a review of the biography of John Quinn in the *New York Times* that the original manuscript of T.S. Eliot's *The Waste Land* survived in the New York Public Library. For years I had been telling my graduate students that any one of them could make his reputation by locating the lost manuscript—and I thought I was suggesting an impossible task, that the manuscript was permanently lost, probably destroyed.

All my life—or so it seemed—I had been learning to live with *The Waste Land*. I must confess that I resisted it at first, but it was not long before I realized that the poem infected the way I looked at the world. Lines popped into my mind at the oddest moments, in the unlikeliest of places: "April is the cruellest month, breeding/ Lilacs out of the dead land . . . "; "Hurry up please it's time"; " . . . the young man carbuncular . . . "; "Consider Phlebas, who was once handsome and tall as you"; "These fragments I have shored against my ruins." *These* and other fragments lodged themselves deep in my psyche, and no doubt shaped my vision of experience, of the world. Moreover, Eliot's criticism, or what Cleanth Brooks and Robert Penn

Warren and others made of it, shaped the way I had looked at literature. In the New Criticism, Eliot was God and Brooks was his prophet. And among the many dogmas of the faith were three of the first importance: an absolute divorce between biography and literature, because of the interposition of something called the "objective correlative"; a denial that poetry was an expression of emotion, or even "emotion recollected in tranquility," but was something quite different, characterized more by irony than emotion; and rejection of poetry as idea, a poem as a statement that might be reduced to a sequence of assertions in the sinful practice known as the heresy of paraphrase. These formulas are perhaps somewhat too simple, but they suggest the way Eliot through both his poetry and his criticism shaped several generations of readers and critics.

Now *The Waste Land* seemed to live up to the first two tenets of the New Criticism admirably. It appeared to be the last poem in the world that could be read biographically; it seemed to be highly restrained and oblique emotionally, filled with irony. But it was paraphrased to a fare-thee-well by many heretics, among them some of the truest of the true believers. Even Cleanth Brooks in one of his most famous essays told us what the poem stated about the world. Indeed, even though obscure debates continued through the decades about the various meanings of *The Waste Land*, detailed, line by line, passage by passage, there gradually developed what seemed like universal agreement that the poem was a pessimistic statement about the modern world, an assertion that modern man lived a futile life in a meaningless world in which all faiths and beliefs had been reduced to a heap of enigmatic fragments. This apocalyptic vision of a world become waste land seemed both to embody and to express the bleak views of several generations of intellectuals and artists. As the poem became overly familiar through over-use, it was reduced to a kind of shorthand way of making references to modern life. And modern life seemed to oblige in remarkable ways, by confirming the simple observation that it was indeed a waste land—air pollution, garbage heaps, chemical poisons, plastics that would not disintegrate, physical and moral corruption that stunned the senses and the mind.

This was the situation in effect when, some fifty years after the initial publication of *The Waste Land*, the (or *a*) manuscript version was published, with full descriptions of Ezra Pound's recommendations for revision. The critical question that seemed to hang in the balance was whether this publication would change the way we read the 1922 version of the poem. Valerie Eliot, who edited the manuscript version, seemed to suggest such a change would reflect more closely Eliot's own notion of the meaning of his poem. She placed as epigraph to her edition Eliot's own statement: "Various critics have done me the honour to interpret the poem in terms of criticism of the contemporary world, have considered it, indeed, as an important bit of social criticism. To me it was only the relief of a personal and wholly insignificant grouse against life; it is just a piece of rhythmical grumbling."[1] Although the instinct of many readers was to discount this statement, and even to point to the vagueness of its origins (it was quoted by someone who heard it at a lecture, and recorded by a third party), it is, in fact, quite in keeping with an entire series of such statements made by Eliot in public and for the record. In 1931, in "Thoughts after Lambeth": "When I wrote a poem called *The Waste Land* some of the more approving critics said that I had expressed the 'disillusionment of a generation,' which is nonsense. I may have expressed for them their own illusion of being disillusioned, but that did not form part of my intention."[2] When, in a 1959 *Paris Review* interview, Eliot was pressed on this statement, he in effect reaffirmed it: "No, it wasn't part of my conscious intention. I think that in 'Thoughts after Lambeth,' I was speaking of intentions more in a negative than in a positive sense, to say what was not my intention. I wonder what an 'intention' means! One wants to get something off one's chest. One doesn't know quite what it is that one wants to get off the chest until one's got it off." It was later in this same interview that Eliot made the astonishing statement (when asked to compare his two long poems): "By the time of the *Four Quartets*, I couldn't have written in the style of *The Waste Land*. In *The Waste Land*, I wasn't even bothering whether I understood what I was saying. These things, however, become easier to people with time. You get used to having *The Waste Land*, or *Ulysses*, about."[3]

Other examples of similar statements by Eliot about *The Waste Land* abound. In *The Use of Poetry and the Use of Criticism* (1933; based on the Charles Eliot Norton lectures at Harvard, 1932–33), he said, as noted in the preface, that "what a poem means is as much what it means to others as what it means to the author," and added that the poet may become "merely a reader" of his own works—"forgetting his original meaning—or without forgetting, merely changing."[4] In his 1951 lecture on "Virgil and the Christian World," Eliot made perhaps his most intriguing statement about *The Waste Land* without naming the poem: "A poet may believe that he is expressing only his private experience; his lines may be for him only a means of talking about himself without giving himself away; yet for his readers what he has written may come to be the expression both of their own secret feelings and of the exultation or despair of a generation. He need not know what his poetry will come to mean to others; and a prophet need not understand the meaning of his prophetic utterance."[5]

In all these statements, direct and oblique, about *The Waste Land*, Eliot emphasizes more and more the personal, private matter that went into the poem, and his astonishment at the way the poem came to be read (a way in which he finally acquiesced, even while insisting that it was not part of his intention) as a public statement about the modern world. In the last of the comments quoted above, he has perhaps put his feelings in their most extreme language. Could it possibly be that Eliot believed that in *The Waste Land* he was "expressing only his private experience"? That the lines of this most famous poem of the twentieth century were for the author "only a means of talking about himself without giving himself away"? *Giving himself away?* Giving what away? What was there to conceal? What, presumably, nobody had, by the 1951 lecture, discovered, or at least discovered and revealed. Could it be that the 1917 essay "Tradition and the Individual Talent," with its elaborate and tortured "impersonal theory" of poetry, had been a sophistic or sophisticated defense for someone wanting to write poetry "talking about himself without giving himself away"?

We might assume that with the publication in 1971 of *The Waste Land* manuscripts Eliot's statements about his poem might have challenged reviewers and critics to find out what he meant, to look for clues for the concealed private experience. By and large, the commentators on the poem, many of them a part of the critical establishment with vested interests in the received "public" reading of *The Waste Land*, found renewed confirmation of the traditional reading, and expressed their admiration for Ezra Pound's skill in revising and radically cutting the poem. There were some who made some limited gestures to define the personal content of the poem as revealed by the manuscripts, but no very persuasive new reading seemed to emerge from the publication.

It is at this point that I want myself to turn personal and describe what is perhaps a revealing narrative, at least as I experienced it. Having reached pretty much the state of mind described in the foregoing paragraphs, I was only recently (spring 1974) urging my students in a seminar in American poetry to try a new reading of the original *Waste Land*, with renewed attention to Eliot's various statements. My exhortations had not come to much in previous classes, and I did not expect too much this time. I spent some time in class suggesting that one way of reading the poem as in some sense personal would be to focus not on the relation of the imagery to the world but rather on the relation of the imagery to the state of mind of a "speaker" or "meditator." Indeed, what kind of person might we imagine this speaker to be, given the nature of the imagery, particularly the sexual imagery with all its apparent revulsion at sexuality? Could we characterize the speaker not simply (as usual) as a sensitive man perceiving the world as it is, but rather as a speaker with deeply disabling inhibitions about sex, certain deeply ingrained revulsions and repressions—someone, say, like J. Alfred Prufrock, seeing the world through the distorting lenses of his disturbed psyche? What if, I challenged, we assumed that Prufrock or someone similar (more or less) were the consciousness of the poem—what would that do to the traditional "public" interpretation? What might we make of the personal content of the poem, especially in view of the rich resources provided by the manuscripts? (And, for that matter, what if "The Love Song of J. Alfred Prufrock" didn't have its title? Would the poem be read as public comment?)

It was shortly after some such commentary in class that I happened to glance over some of the footnotes in Robert Sencourt's biography *T.S. Eliot: A Memoir*. I do not remember what, if anything, I was looking for, but my eye alighted on footnote 7, Chapter 3: "Jean Verdenal, as Phlebas the Phoenician, has left a profound imprint on *The Waste Land*. Cf. J. Peter's thoughtful and constructive essay, 'A New Interpretation of *The Waste Land*,' *Essays in Criticism*."[6]

My distaste for certain obvious aspects of the Sencourt book did not entirely dissipate my curiosity about such a strange footnote: even though I had read a great quantity of criticism on *The Waste Land*, owned several casebooks that claimed to cover the major lines of debate on the poem, and had even browsed through bibliographies of works on the poem, I had never encountered an essay suggesting a live counterpart for Phlebas the Phoenician. Moreover, all my instincts, largely shaped by the Eliot-created New Criticism, were against such reductive kinds of identifications as leading to non-interpretations.

Nevertheless, I sought out the John Peter essay and began to read it—with considerable astonishment. It presented a reading of *The Waste Land* so close to the kind that I had just been calling for in class that I was amazed. Early in the essay, Peter outlined his reading of the poem: "At some previous time the speaker has fallen completely— perhaps the right word is 'irretrievably'—in love. The object of this love was a young man who soon afterwards met his death, it would seem by drowning. Enough time has now elapsed since his death for the speaker to have realized that the focus for affection that he once provided is irreplaceable. The monologue which, in effect, the poem presents is a meditation upon this deprivation, upon the speaker's stunned and horrified reactions to it, and on the picture which, as seen through its all but insupportable bleakness, the world presents."[7] This outline of the "argument" of *The Waste Land* is breathtaking in its simplicity and almost defiant in its specificity. When I had urged my students to attempt a reading that would recreate the consciousness of the speaker, I did not believe that there was enough evidence in the poem to recreate so specifically the dramatic situation of the speaker. Even though I read the Peter article with some skepticism as to the specifics, my admiration grew for the consistence in his exploration of a nonpublic interpretation, his sketching of a genuinely dramatic reading. In short, he read the poem, without reference to biography (with no identification of Phlebas the Phoenician), rather much as a variation in kind of "The Love Song of J. Alfred Prufrock"—a dramatic meditation, vividly recreating the imagistic flow of a mind in delicate psychic balance—or unbalance.

My personal narrative must now turn bibliographic, a mode usually fraught with profound dullness, but one which I found this time of the utmost fascination. John Peter's article was first published in *Essays in Criticism* in July 1952 (pp. 242–66). But not all copies of that issue contain the essay, for the simple reason that they were confiscated and destroyed as a result of solicitors acting on behalf of their client, none other than T.S. Eliot himself. The startling and perhaps revealing story of this event is told in *Essays in Criticism* for April 1969 (recall that Eliot died in 1965), in which issue the Peter article is republished together with a most interesting "Postscript." This "Postscript" (in addition to identifying Eliot's Phlebas the Phoenician as one Jean Verdenal) gives an account of John Peter (who referred to himself as "an impecunious junior professor in the Canadian Middle West") tendering an apology to Eliot through the solicitors, and the acceptance of the apology by Eliot—but together with the indication that "he considered it neither necessary nor desirable for a public retraction to appear." The solicitors assured John Peter that "their client would 'take the very gravest view of any further dissemination of this article or the views expressed in it.' "[8]

In reporting his experience with Eliot in the "Postscript" to his article, John Peter quotes his correspondence from the poet's solicitors only once. They informed Peter that Eliot had read his essay "with amazement and disgust," and that it was "absurd" and "completely erroneous" (p. 173). It is of interest to remember that this is the same poet who, some seven years later, would tell his *Paris Review* interviewer that in writing *The Waste Land* he "wasn't even bothering" whether he "understood what he was saying."

From the time of the first publication and suppression of the John Peter essay in 1952 until its republication with the "Postscript" in 1969, a period of some seventeen years, Eliot scholarship and criticism accumulated at a prodigious rate—but with what almost seems a conspiracy of silence on the Peter essay. But, in breaking silence in 1969, John Peter did more than tell of the suppression of his essay. He added about ten pages of biographical speculation that went far beyond his original essay in suggesting *The Waste Land* was indeed a very *personal* poem. Not only did he identify Jean Verdenal as providing the basis for Phlebas the Phoenician, but he presented a good deal of evidence, some of it highly conjectural and tenuous, to support his autobiographical reading of the poem. Thus John Peter's work stands curiously divided, the basic essay (dating from 1952)

arguing not a personal but a dramatic (as opposed to a public) interpretation, with the consciousness of *The Waste Land* always carefully
removed from identification with Eliot; and the "Postscript" (dating
from 1969) arguing a personal (as opposed to a dramatic) interpretation of the poem based on direct biographical data, some quite
elusive.

When I first came across, almost by accident, the John Peter story,
I accused myself of carelessness in having missed it for so long—but
then, I consoled myself, I have never tried to keep up with the flood
of Eliot commentary inasmuch as my critical interests have run in
other directions. Even so, however, I *did* teach *The Waste Land*, and I
felt I had been forgoing a fascinating part of the story of its reputation that would naturally arouse student interest. I then began to
check how I had overlooked it. I immediately pulled eight critical
volumes from my own Eliot shelf, all of which are widely circulated
guides, handbooks, and interpretations, and three of which are devoted entirely to *The Waste Land*, bringing together essays by various
hands. Not one—not a single one—of these books made mention of
John Peter or his essay or theory, and neither did his essay get listed
in the selected bibliographies—not even in the *Waste Land* casebooks!
Realizing that my Eliot library was limited, I made a quick check of
other books dealing with *The Waste Land* in the University of Chicago
library, and found almost total silence on the Peter article. I did find,
however, this brief sentence in the "Introduction" to one casebook
on *The Waste Land*: "In *Essays in Criticism* (1952), John Peter had
emphasized the poet's revulsion from sexual relationships in a controversial article we have not been allowed to reprint."[9] Although
this sentence is curiously reticent in its description, it does explain
the non-appearance of the Peter essay, but not its absence from
bibliographies nor the silence on its controversial thesis in commentary by others.

With the reprinting of the Peter essay in 1969 together with the
remarkable "Postscript," and the arrival of a time when the essay no
longer faced legal challenge, we might expect to find more receptiv-
ity to it in the critical literature. Indeed, with the publication of the
Waste Land manuscripts in 1971, and the new discussions begun then
and still going on about this most famous of modern poems, we
might look for either challenge, confirmation, or refutation of Peter's

controversial ideas. But the reviews and the continuing critical commentary, even though often stressing that the manuscripts reveal
more personal emphasis than the Pound-revised poem, appear to
remain obtuse about John Peter and his notions, treating them very
gingerly when touching on them at all. If what prevails is not exactly
a conspiracy of silence, it certainly is not an open discussion of interesting interpretive ideas. Of course, many of the reviewers and recent commentators are identical with the earlier, and have vested
interests in established interpretive positions.

There is one important exception to my generalization about the
reviews of *The Waste Land* manuscripts: the review which appeared
in the London *Times Literary Supplement,* 10 December 1971: "T.S.
Eliot and the 'Out There.' " This review, noting Eliot's repeated
insistence that *The Waste Land* was a personal poem, proposed a new
way of seeing the poem: "The point [in the poem] is neither the
emotion felt and expressed, nor the 'out there' which appears (mis-
leadingly) to provoke or to focus that emotion; the point of interest
which determines the poem's structure is somewhere between the
emotion and its apparent object or provocation—it is 'the nerves in
patterns' "(p. 1551). But the review notes that the manuscripts of *The
Waste Land* (particularly the Fresca couplets) confirm what many
critics had already charged—that a powerful emotion behind the
poem is the "hatred and fear of sex." After noting that the misogyny
of *The Waste Land* aligns it "with the ancient tradition of Juvenal and
Dryden, Pope and Swift, the poems written by men against women,
and against the sexual enslavement to which the mere fact of
Woman condemns most men," the reviewer then suggests: "Let us
come to terms, as best we can, with the fact that the most influential
English poem of our time was impelled by a hatred and fear (oh yes,
that much we have learnt—hatred, and therefore fear) of woman as
a sexual partner. It could be the occasion for a quite momentous
clearing of our minds of cant" (p. 1552).

Although the momentous "occasion" the reviewer envisioned did
not materialize, there was a minor tempest in a small teapot that
endured through the months of January and February 1972, in the
"To the Editor" column of the *Times Literary Supplement.* I.A. Richards began the exchange on 14 January 1972, with a letter of protest
against the review's lament that Eliot had sealed his papers from

unwanted biographers: "Why should not any writer decide not to help those who cannot (to echo Coleridge) subordinate their curiosities about the poet to their sympathy with the poetry" (p. 3646). G. Wilson Knight entered the fray in the same issue with a letter pointing to evidence in the *Waste Land* manuscripts that the "hyacinth girl" ("the key to *The Waste Land*") was not really female. This and other revelations of the manuscripts led him to conclude: "that Eliot's poetry—I make no statement regarding his life—should contain a reference to what I call the 'seraphic' vision need hardly disturb us. It simply means that he was a real poet."[10]

Letters in the *Times Literary Supplement* continued to debate the meaning of *The Waste Land* for several more issues, and included as correspondents Anne Ridler, Helen Gardner, H.Z. Maccoby, and others, with G. Wilson Knight making several appearances.[11] More voices were raised in support of Richards' sentiments than in support of Knight's analyses. It was not until the 11 February 1972 issue that David R. Rebmann reminded the participants (and readers) that John Peter had addressed himself to many of the issues being debated in the articles in *Essays in Criticism* discussed above. But the summary of Peter's theories about the poem elicited more attack than support, and the controversy trailed off inconclusively. It seems fairly clear that no one had changed his position because of the arguments offered in the letters. And the arguments did not seem to long survive the swiftly disappearing pages of the *TLS*. Subsequent essays in the little magazines and learned journals seem mostly to have been written without awareness of the issues so hotly joined in this brief flare-up of discussion.

Among other reviews of the *Waste Land* manuscripts, it comes as something of a surprise to happen upon Frank Kermode's comment in *The Atlantic Monthly*: "The homosexual interpretation of *The Waste Land,* which is quite fashionable, gains no new support, and indeed seems even more gratuitous."[12] Fashionable? Where? In the halls and rooms of sequestered universities? Kermode makes no mention of John Peter here. And more grievously, he misstates the case. The language, "homosexual interpretation," seems deliberately designed to jar the sensibility and provoke negative vibrations; and whatever this interpretation might be called, there is a good deal more support for it in the *Waste Land* manuscripts than Kermode admits.

3

Faint Clews and Indirections

The Sub-Surface Life

Why even I myself I often think know little or nothing of my real
  life,
Only a few hints, a few diffused faint clews and indirections
Walt Whitman

In the face of Eliot's recorded hostility toward biography, it may
seem foolhardy to venture into the privacy of the poet. But others
have ventured there before, and largely without the help of those
who control the source materials. The basic biographical questions
we would like answered: who was Jean Verdenal, and what was his
relationship with Eliot? Eliot himself provided some evidence, mostly
mysterious. Eliot dedicated his first volume of poems, *Prufrock and
Other Observations* (1917), "To Jean Verdenal/1889–1915." At the
front of his 1920 volume of poems entitled *Ara Vos Prec*, published
in England in a small edition, there was no dedication but an epigraph from Canto XXI, 133–36, of Dante's *Purgatorio:*

> Or puoi, la quantitate
> Comprender dell' amor ch'a te mi scalda,
> Quando dismento nostra vanitate
> Trattando l'ombre come cosa salda.

A simple translation:

> Now you are able to comprehend the quantity of love
> that warms me toward you,/ When I forget our emptiness/
> Treating shades as if they were solid.

Ara Vos Prec and one of the poems, "Ode," that appears in it (later suppressed) are discussed in Chapter 5 below. It is sufficient to point out here the oddity of what appeared to be a dedicatory epigraph appearing with no indication of the individual to whom the volume is dedicated. When the American edition of this collection of poems appeared (with "Hysteria" replacing "Ode"), also in 1920, there was no epigraph but a dedication identical to that in the *Prufrock* volume: "To Jean Verdenal/1889–1915." It was not until Eliot's *Poems: 1909–1925* appeared in 1925 that the dedication to Jean Verdenal (with the additional informative line, *mort aux Dardanelles)* and the Dante epigraph came together, standing at the head of the poems of the *Prufrock* volume as a unit (the book itself was dedicated to the poet's father, Henry Ware Eliot, who had died in 1919). Subsequent publication of Eliot's collected poems carried this dedication and epigraph attached to the *Prufrock* poems. It is of interest to note that Eliot waited until 1925 to bring together this ardent dedication and the name of Jean Verdenal, and that once they found a place in his poems, they remained there permanently.

"Now you are able to comprehend the quantity of love that warms me toward you,/ When I forget our emptiness/ Treating shades as if they were solid." The words are spoken in the *Purgatorio* by the dead poet Statius (author of *Thebaid*) to Virgil as he accompanies Dante. The source of the quote does not provide much illumination, but the warmth and intensity of the dedication does, perhaps, take on added meaning in the context of the poems that it finally became closely attached to—"The Love Song of J. Alfred Prufrock" and "Portrait of a Lady" (among others), poems that dramatize the speaker's paralysis of sexual feeling in relations with women.

The only other public reference by Eliot to Jean Verdenal appeared some seventeen years after the *Prufrock* dedication, in the April 1934 issue of *The Criterion,* in the editor's column, "A Commentary." In browsing through a book (Henry Massis, *Evocations,* 1931) about Paris during the time that Eliot was a student at the Sorbonne there (1910–11), Eliot becomes steeped in romantic memories, and turns both autobiographical and confessional, as, in an aside, he says: "I am willing to admit that my own retrospect is touched by a sentimental sunset, the memory of a friend coming across the Luxembourg Gardens in the late afternoon, waving a branch of lilac, a friend who was later (so far as I could find out) to be mixed with the mud of Gallipoli."[1] This brief comment stands out with remarkable brilliancy in the brief "Commentary," as it is the only genuinely personal note struck in what is essentially a reminiscence of the intellectual and literary milieu of Paris during Eliot's year there a quarter of a century before. Although Jean Verdenal's name is not mentioned, there seems little doubt in view of the *Prufrock* dedication that he is the friend referred to.

What more can we find out about Jean Verdenal? We might look to the biographical volumes on Eliot to find out what we can. The one book that was compiled while Eliot was still alive, Herbert Howarth's *Notes on Some Figures Behind T.S. Eliot* (1965), covers in some detail Eliot's student year in Paris, but does not make a single reference to Jean Verdenal. Since Eliot's death in 1965 up to this writing (1974), some four books might qualify for the title of biography. Two of these are in the nature of intellectual biographies whose authors seem not to have been ambitious in accumulating data about the private or personal life. Russell Kirk, in *Eliot and His Age* (1971), quotes the "Commentary" passage from the 1934 *Criterion* mentioned above, but makes no attempt to identify the friend, and does not mention Jean Verdenal elsewhere in his book. Bernard Bergonzi, in *T.S. Eliot* (1972), notes the *Criterion* quote, connects it with the *Prufrock* dedication, and refers to Jean Verdenal only as a "shadowy figure from Eliot's period in Paris."[2]

The other two biographical volumes attempt to delve much more deeply into the personal life of Eliot, working against Eliot's will and clearly without the cooperation of Eliot's widow and literary executor, Valerie Eliot. It is a pity that both books have been written by men so insensitive to the biographical and literary materials, for they have braved what others have not dared in defying the poet's wishes and his widow. But their immature judgments and lapses in taste make it woefully obvious that they qualify for neither of the avocations Eliot specified for the writer of a literary biography—criticism and psychology (see Chapter 4). Robert Sencourt's *T.S. Eliot: A Memoir* (1971) is the most offensive in its pretense to a familiarity with Eliot that is both cloying and obviously to a large extent manufactured. But Sencourt (who died in 1969) brought together for the first time a good deal of scattered material which may be valuable if used with care. In writing of Eliot's Paris days, he says: "The friend whose memory lingered longest with him was a medical student, Jean Verdenal, who in a life tragically cut short at Gallipoli also found time to be a poet. In letters at the Houghton Library, Harvard, I found the record of this affinity of hearts." In a footnote to this passage, Sencourt adds the reference to the John Peter essay (mentioning the identification of Phlebas the Phoenician with Jean Verdenal) referred to above. The most recent biography of Eliot, T.S. Matthews' *Great Tom: Notes Toward the Definition of T.S. Eliot* (1974), reviews the scarce data, notes that Eliot and Verdenal lived in the same *pension* in Paris during 1910–11, and then observes: "What are we to make of these facts? Not much, beyond inferring that a friendship between young men can be warm and may stir the blood without firing it, and that there may well have been some exaggeration in Eliot's melancholy remembrance of this foreign friend."[3] Matthews remains silent on the John Peter article and the legal action Eliot took in 1952 against it.

Intrigued by Robert Sencourt's reference to the letters from Jean Verdenal to Eliot in the Houghton Library at Harvard, I wrote to the Library and was informed that there are indeed seven letters preserved there, but permission to read them must be given by Mrs. T.S. Eliot. I wrote to Mrs. Eliot asking permission to see these letters and also asked her whether she planned to include the letters in her forthcoming edition of Eliot letters. She replied (23 July 1974) that she was planning to include the Verdenal letters in an appendix to the first volume of Eliot's correspondence, that no copies of Eliot's letters to Verdenal survived, and that the Verdenal letters were to be withheld from the public until they appeared in her edition of Eliot's letters.

In the summer of 1976, George Watson published in *The Sewanee Review* his "Quest for a Frenchman,"[4] presenting what he was able to discover about Jean Verdenal through French military records and talks with a younger brother (Pierre Verdenal) and with a surviving friend. The service records revealed that Jean was born not in 1889 as Eliot indicated in his dedication but in 1890 (11 May). Verdenal entered military service in March 1913, and "became a medical of-

ficer in November 1914." The record indicates that he was "killed by
the enemy on the 2nd May 1915 in the Dardanelles," and contains a
citation dated 30 April 1915: "Scarcely recovered from pleurisy, he
did not hesitate to spend much of the night in the water up to his
waist helping to evacuate the wounded by sea, thus giving a notable
example of self-sacrifice." And a later entry in the record, dated 23
June 1915, says: "Verdenal, assistant medical officer, performed his
duties with courage and devotion. He was killed on the 2nd May
1915 while dressing a wounded man on the field of battle" (p. 467).
Visits with Verdenal's brother Pierre revealed that Jean had in his
library volumes of Mallarmé and Laforgue. Visits with Verdenal's
friend Dr. André Schlemmer revealed that Jean "took a small interest" in Charles Maurras and his *Action Française,* an interest that Eliot
manifested later (pp. 469–72).

George Watson concluded: "I believe Eliot's debt to Verdenal was
in the conversation he gave and the literary acquaintance he offered.
All this, no doubt, warmed by a profound and admiring affection
that may rightly be called love" (p. 474). But it is questionable as to
whether Watson's discoveries, important as they are, can be taken as
definitive (as he assumes) in demonstrating that Verdenal could not
be related to Phlebas the Phoenician. The chaos of the battles fought
from the ships and on the shores of Gallipoli in 1915 (and as reflected in Verdenal's own service record) inevitably guaranteed con-
fusion about the disposition of the battle dead. And Eliot's 1934
statement—that as far as he "could find out," Verdenal had been
"mixed with the mud of Gallipoli"—is an ambiguous remark show-
ing that he was never sure of his friend's fate. Moreover, Eliot's
transfiguring imagination was capable of changing details of fact
while leaving intact intensities of feeling. And finally, there are in
The Waste Land many images of death "by land" as well as "by water,"
including, for example, what could be taken as a Gallipoli scene of
mud and rats near the beginning of "The Fire Sermon": "White
bodies naked on the low damp ground." Verdenal's haunting presence in *The Waste Land* is not ultimately dependent on a literal identification of his fate with that of Phlebas the Phoenician.

A quick survey of Eliot's years after Paris is helpful: Eliot went to
London in 1914, after first visiting France (where it is possible he
could have seen Verdenal again, even though his friend was by this
time in service), and then Marburg, Germany, which he was forced
to leave because of the advent of World War I. In a seemingly

sudden civil ceremony on 26 June 1915, Eliot married Vivienne
Haigh-Wood in Hampstead, a marriage "encouraged" (Valerie Eliot
indicates[5]) by Ezra Pound. We may assume that this marriage took
place after Eliot learned of Verdenal's death in the Dardanelles. The
puzzling aspects of this marriage are best suggested in a letter written by Bertrand Russell in July 1915, only a month or so after the
marriage: "I dined with my Harvard pupil, [T.S.] Eliot, and his
bride. I expected her to be terrible, from his mysteriousness; but she
was not so bad. She is light, a little vulgar, adventurous, full of life—
an artist I think he said, but I should have thought her an actress.
He is exquisite and listless; she says she married him to stimulate
him, but finds she can't do it. Obviously he married in order to be
stimulated. I think she will soon be tired of him. She refuses to go to
America to see his people, for fear of submarines. He is ashamed of
his marriage, and very grateful if one is kind to her. He is the Miss
Sands type of American." Russell's footnote explains that "Miss
Sands was a highly cultivated New Englander, a painter and a friend
of Henry James and Logan Pearsall Smith" (p. 61).[6]

In January 1916, Bertrand Russell, friend of the Eliots and well-
known collector of mistresses, took Vivienne off alone to Torquay
for a seaside holiday, while Eliot stayed in London. Russell's developing interest in Vivienne is apparent in his letters. In a November
1915 letter he notes that she has "impulses of cruelty to him [Eliot]
from time to time. It is a Dostojevsky type of cruelty, not a
straightforward everyday kind. I am every day getting things more
right between them, but I can't let them alone at present, and of
course I myself get very much interested. She is a person who lives
on a knife-edge, and will end as a criminal or a saint—I don't know
which yet. She has a perfect capacity for both"(p. 64). In a January
1916 letter, Eliot thanked Russell effusively for taking Vivienne on
the seaside vacation: "I am sure you have done *everything* possible,
and handled her in the very best way; better than I. . . . I believe we
shall owe her life to you, even" (pp. 67–68). How precisely did Russell, notorious for his sexual exploits and capacities during this period, help Vivienne Eliot; and what precisely is the nature of T.S.
Eliot's gratefulness? In a September 1916 letter to his on-again, off-
again mistress of that period, Russell wrote: "I shall soon have come
to the end of the readjustment with Mrs. E. [Mrs. T.S. Eliot]. I think
it will be all right, on a better basis. As soon as it is settled, I will
come to Garsington. I long to come. . . . I had a sense of success with

Mrs. E. because I achieved what I meant to achieve (which was not so very difficult) but now I have lost that, not by your fault in the least. The sense of success helps my work: when I lose it my writing grows dull and lifeless" (pp. 93–94). Clearly who was helping (or using) whom in this Bertrand Russell-Vivienne Eliot relationship remains a live question.

In a state near nervous collapse in late 1921, Eliot took leave from his bank job in September and went first to Margate, with Vivienne, and later—alone—to Switzerland to see a psychiatrist recommended by Bertrand Russell's mistress, Lady Ottaline Morrell, and also by Julian Huxley—one Roger Vittoz (see discussion of essay by psychiatrist Harry Trosman, below). He was in Lausanne about six weeks and wrote there (or finished writing) *The Waste Land,* gave the (or *a*) manuscript to Ezra Pound in December, and, after following most of Pound's suggestions for revision of the poem, published it in October 1922, in both *The Criterion* in England and *The Dial* in America. During the years from his marriage to this collapse, his letters (as quoted by Valerie Eliot in her introduction to the *Waste Land* manuscripts) indicate that he was finding it difficult if not impossible to write poetry. In a letter to Richard Aldington (6 November 1921) he commented on his own state of health, saying that his "nerves" were "due not to overwork but to an aboulie [lack of will] and emotional derangement which has been a lifelong affliction. Nothing wrong with my mind—."[7] In a footnote to Part V ("What the Thunder Said") in the published manuscripts of *The Waste Land,* Valerie Eliot writes: "Eliot said that he was describing his own experience of writing this section in Lausanne when he wrote in *The 'Pensees' of Pascal* (1931): ' . . . it is a commonplace that some forms of illness are extremely favourable, not only to religious illumination, but to artistic and literary composition. A piece of writing meditated, apparently without progress for months or years, may suddenly take shape and work; and in this state long passages may be produced which require little or no retouch.' "[8]

It is worthwhile to review briefly the facts just outlined: in 1910, at the age of 22, Eliot went to Paris and found living in his *pension* a charming young Frenchman, age 20, who was studying medicine and who read and wrote poetry. Loneliness guided Eliot into a warm friendship. It would have been natural for the two to travel in Italy and Germany during the summer of 1911 (it was in Munich that Eliot finished "The Love Song of J. Alfred Prufrock"), and it is possible that their relationship was briefly renewed in 1914 on Eliot's return to Paris (if Verdenal's service had not made a visit impossible). World War I forced Eliot's departure from Germany to England in 1914, and led to Verdenal's service as medical officer in the French forces. Caught up in the campaign to take the Dardanelles in 1915, he was one of the countless young Frenchmen, Englishmen, and Australians who were lost in the waters of the Strait and the mud of Gallipoli during and after the landings of 24 April 1915: he was killed on the battlefield on 2 May. Eliot would have heard of Verdenal's death in May or June, and his dismay and anguish—or complex emotions only a psychiatrist could disentangle—may well have impelled him into a hasty marriage on 26 June that was largely meaningless except as an irrational response to his bitter loss. The marriage turned out to be catastrophic, apparently without satisfaction for either partner; and Eliot appeared grateful, only some six months after the marriage, when the well-known satyr Bertrand Russell took his recent bride off on a seaside holiday alone. But as Vivienne's mental health deteriorated, perhaps in part through the frustrations stemming from her unsatisfying marriage, T.S. Eliot's health began to deteriorate and his ability to write poetry to decline. The critical point was reached in 1921, when he found his only refuge from a breakdown was to take leave from his job, consult a nerve specialist, or psychiatrist, in Lausanne, and write a long poem which had been under contemplation for some time—*The Waste Land.*

That long poem, when it was finally to appear, would open:

> April is the cruellest month, breeding
> Lilacs out of the dead land, mixing
> Memory and desire

Was April cruel because it was perhaps associated with the Gallipoli landings and Verdenal's death? And April brought the cruel reminder of lilacs: in 1934, Eliot's memory of the Paris of 1910 was symbolized by the romantic image of Verdenal waving a branch of lilac. Eliot had, in earlier poetry, used the image of lilacs to suggest sensual allurement—in "Portrait of a Lady" (1917), at the opening of Part II—

Now that lilacs are in bloom
She has a bowl of lilacs in her room
And twists one in her fingers while she talks.

And Eliot would return to the haunting image of the lilac as a symbol of physical temptation in Part III of "Ash-Wednesday" (1930):

Blown hair is sweet, brown hair over the mouth blown,
Lilac and brown hair

When in his 1934 recollection of the Paris of his student days, Eliot summoned up, in what seems like an almost involuntary outburst of personal anguish, the image of Jean Verdenal with the branch of lilac, he was surely recalling more than a city, more than a historic moment. That branch of lilac evidently bore a heavy weight of association, "mixing/ Memory and desire."

We know that Eliot's memory of Jean Verdenal was marked by romantic elements—a sunset at the Luxembourg Gardens, a branch of lilacs, a keen pang of loss. What was his memory of Vivienne, married in haste, thrust in apparent offering at Bertrand Russell, tolerated for a time, eventually (in the early 1930s) utterly abandoned? Maybe one day letters or other records will come to light and illuminate the obscurity. In the meantime, what have Eliot's biographers made of Vivienne? They have offered strangely conflicting speculation about the abruptness of the marriage.

Russell Kirk found it simply an inexplicable error: "By 1915, at the age of twenty-seven, T.S. Eliot had made only one grave mistake in his life, but that very grave: his marriage. . . . Vivienne Haigh-Wood suffered from poor health, from obscure neuroses, and, in the judgment of several, from vulgarity."[9] Bernard Bergonzi writes of Eliot's marriage: "It was to cause him much unhappiness and appears to have reinforced rather than assuaged the sexual anxieties expressed in his early poetry. Little is known about the course of Eliot's marriage, save for a few hints dropped by his friends and contemporaries about the intensity of his private suffering."[10] Robert Sencourt, perhaps the most vitriolic Vivienne analyst of all the biographers, apparently thought he found the secret of her misery-dispensing power in the peculiar or perverse charms of her femininity: "Essential to her vivacious nature was her mingling of sparkle and sensitiveness with the sardonic and playful. This was the secret of her undeniable seductiveness. . . . It is normal for a woman to enjoy her power to play upon the strings and nerves of manhood till they hasten the throbbing pulse with sensations of peculiar pleasure."[11] But if Sencourt suggests that Vivienne seduced Eliot, T.S. Matthews toys with the notion that Eliot "compromised" her—he playing the "young man carbuncular," she the "indifferent typist." But Matthews does not fully commit himself to this theory, and concludes: "The Eliots' marriage was unhappy, as everyone within miles of it was aware. But how to define the unhappiness of this particular marriage?"[12]

In addition to the full-length biographies of Eliot there have begun to appear psychoanalytic essays which stress Eliot's marriage in an attempt to provide a sound biographical approach to Eliot's poetry. Two of these must be mentioned: George Whiteside's "T.S. Eliot: The Psychobiographical Approach" (1973) and Harry Trosman's "T.S. Eliot and *The Waste Land:* Psychopathological Antecedents and Transformations" (1974). Whiteside's essay does not, astonishingly, mention Jean Verdenal, but hypothesizes that the causes for Eliot's deteriorating relationship with his wife Vivienne were to be found in his ties to his parents, and particularly in some traumatic early experience involving his mother which disabled the son in all subsequent female relationships: "I think Eliot's feeling that the instinctual urges in men are violent was a schizoid feeling but also goes a long way to explain his fear of sex. Sex to him seemed (at least until his second marriage) to be a violent business and, in particular, one that involved not people but merely urges and therefore involved merely parts of bodies."[13] Whiteside gives much of his essay over to analyzing Eliot's poetry psychobiographically, and is most persuasive in dealing with a work like the prose-poem "Hysteria" as growing out of an actual experience with Vivienne.

Although Harry Trosman, in his psychopathological approach, does mention Jean Verdenal, he does not link Verdenal with Eliot's marriage or illness, nor does he see Verdenal as an important factor in the composition of *The Waste Land.* Dr. Trosman (a psychiatrist) places great emphasis on the death of Eliot's father in 1919, and the visit Eliot's mother paid the Eliots in England in 1921, in tracing the

causes of Eliot's 1921 illness that led to his treatment in Lausanne
and the writing of *The Waste Land*: "His illness can be characterized
as a transitory narcissistic regression with partial fragmentation and
loss of ego dominance." But of course Eliot's relation with Vivienne
was central: "The difficult relationship with Vivienne served as a
constant reminder of sexual failure. Eliot's tolerance for and complicity in Vivienne's affair with Russell suggested an unresolved
oedipal tie and a need to placate a sexually aggressive father surrogate. Vivienne's incipient psychosis aggravated fears of narcissistic
omnipotence and destructiveness."[14] (It should be parenthetically
noted that Dr. Trosman's essay is especially valuable for giving some
background of Roger Vittoz, the Swiss psychiatrist that Eliot con-
sulted in Lausanne, and a description of the treatment that Eliot
probably received from him—a key part of which involved Vittoz's
placing his hand on the forehead of the patient in order to feel the
vibrations of the "cerebral hemispheres.")

The biographers—whether academic, journalistic, or psychoanalytic—make what they can of the strange marriage, but not one of
them attempts to place it in the context of Eliot's relationship with
Jean Verdenal. Moreover, with the stress on Vivienne's "vulgarity," a
word used repeatedly by Eliot's cultivated friends as they remember
their first encounters with her, the biographers from the outset of the
discussion of the marriage take Eliot's side and bestow on him all the
sympathy they withhold from Vivienne. To what extent her "hysteria" (another word that repeatedly appears in the contemporary descriptions of her) might have been caused by Eliot's own problems is
not a subject that the biographers consider. There is every reason to
conclude, especially in view of Eliot's apparent eagerness to send Vivienne off alone with Bertrand Russell, that the poet's marriage was a
sexual failure—whatever the extent of that failure—and that one
cause was his grief for the dead Jean Verdenal (among other factors
in his complex psychological makeup, including his tension-ridden
relationships with his parents as described by Dr. Trosman). Russell's
picture of the listless young Eliot, "ashamed" of his marriage, would
seem to reinforce this conjecture, and the various descriptions of
Vivienne's illness ("hysteria," "nervous disorder," "mental deteriora-
tion") would seem to add further support. In Bertrand Russell's narrative of this period, he writes: "I was fond of them both [the Eliots],

and endeavored to help them in their troubles until I discovered that their troubles were what they enjoyed."[15] This offhand remark may be more penetrating than it seems: perhaps to Russell, Vivienne seemed to enjoy her "troubles" because he was able to give her some satisfaction when he took her off alone; perhaps to Russell in retrospect Eliot seemed to enjoy himself because underneath all his misery he knew deep down in his grief that he was accumulating the materials for a poem, a long poem that might prove to be an enigmatic masterpiece, personal yet impersonal, epic yet anti-epic.

Although Eliot's life after *The Waste Land* is not of primary interest here, it is useful to note the ultimate fate of his marriage. The course of the Eliot marriage continued its downward path through Eliot's religious conversion of 1927 (Vivienne did not share his religious devotions) until their permanent separation in 1933, arranged by solicitors in accordance with previous secret plans while Eliot was in America for a year of lectures. Vivienne's death in 1947 finally freed Eliot from his mysteriously assumed burden. The true story of the relationship will have to wait the advent of someone as patient and meticulous as Nancy Milford, the author of the recent biography *Zelda* (1970), the life of F. Scott Fitzgerald's unhappy wife. The assumption of all the current biographies that Eliot bore the burden of a vulgar, coarse, inferior, and mentally disturbed wife with great forbearance and devotion will surely one day be challenged when it is more fully known to what extent he contributed, however unintentionally, in very deep and psychoanalytic ways to her developing "hysteria." In line with contemporary psychoanalytic theory, Eliot may well have chosen Vivienne because of fears of his own inadequacies and his awareness of her psychological fragility—less threatening than a mature and stable woman. Some time shortly after Vivienne's death (1947), Eliot began to share a London flat with John Hayward, a wheelchair-bound invalid (a victim of muscular dystrophy) who was younger and shared Eliot's interest in language and poetry. When in 1957 Eliot married his Faber and Faber secretary, Valerie Fletcher, his separation from John Hayward was apparently difficult—and apparently planned with as much stealth (and giving rise to as many rumors) as his separation from Vivienne (see the Sencourt and Matthews biographies).

Assembling biographical "facts" and speculating as to what lies behind the blanks does not automatically bestow understanding of the significance of the facts as they become transfigured in the imagination and consciousness of the individual involved. It seems clear that Eliot's experience with Jean Verdenal and Eliot's memory of that experience are two quite different things, and it is necessary for anyone wanting to see Eliot's poetry in the light of Eliot's experience to try to understand the imaginative transfiguration in memory. Eliot himself touched on a similar point in his 1929 essay on Dante, treating the relationship of Dante and Beatrice, finding the meaning not in the "facts" so much as in Dante's *reflection* on his experience with her:

> The attitude of Dante to the fundamental experience of the *Vita Nuova* can only be understood by accustoming ourselves to find meaning in *final causes* rather than in origins. It is not, I believe, meant as a description of what he consciously felt on his meeting with Beatrice, but rather as a description of what that meant on mature reflection upon it. The final cause is the attraction towards God. A great deal of sentiment has been spilt, especially in the eighteenth and nineteenth centuries, upon idealizing the reciprocal feelings of man and woman towards each other, which various realists have been irritated to denounce: this sentiment ignoring the fact that the love of man and woman (or for that matter of man and man) is only explained and made reasonable by the higher love, or else is simply the coupling of animals.[16]

The attentive reader will have surely paused over the parenthetical assertion—"or for that matter of man and man"—as related to the biography we have been at pains to reconstruct. The passage comes in a context in which Eliot is affirming his belief that Dante could have had "the type of sexual experience" at the age of nine (Eliot thinks it might have occurred at an earlier age) that he describes with Beatrice. Eliot goes on (after the above quote): "Let us entertain the theory that Dante, meditating on the astonishment of an experience at such an age, which no subsequent experience abolished or exceeded, found meanings in it which we should not be likely to find ourselves." If we place this statement alongside Eliot's own experiences we have been examining, we might take some measure of the transfiguration Jean Verdenal could have undergone in Eliot's imagination. Of course Eliot was not a child but a young man when he encountered Jean Verdenal; still the experience seems clearly to have been one that "no subsequent experience abolished or exceeded," and one in which *he* "found meanings" far beyond *our* reach when we confine ourselves to the "facts."

To bring this idea into clearer focus, we might take a glance at Eliot's enthusiastic reaction to F. Scott Fitzgerald's *The Great Gatsby*. Fitzgerald sent him an inscribed copy, and Eliot replied (31 December 1925) that he had read it three times, and that it had "interested and excited" him more than any novel for a "number of years." He called *The Great Gatsby* a "remarkable book," and then added the much quoted sentence: "In fact it seems to me to be the first step that American fiction has taken since Henry James."[17] Eliot's reaction might be understood on a number of grounds, but among the most important surely must be listed the strange transformation that the somewhat morally shabby Daisy Buchanan undergoes in Jay Gatsby's incredible imagination. His brief encounter with her fundamentally changes and shapes his life. Gatsby's pursuit of Daisy becomes ultimately the pursuit of the Holy Grail, as his "illusion" assumes a "colossal vitality." The narrator Nick Carroway comments: "No amount of fire or freshness can challenge what a man will store up in his ghostly heart." Of course it is this vitality and freshness that constitutes the core of innocence that Nick finds beneath Gatsby's surface corruption. Gatsby does turn out to be (as Nick observes) the best of the lot of them. And Fitzgerald's novel concludes holding the note of this pervasive theme: "So we beat on, boats against the current, borne back ceaselessly into the past."[18] Eliot must have seen a parallel, with all their differences, between the Gatsby-Daisy and the Dante-Beatrice relationships. And he must himself have vibrated to the novel's lower frequencies as sounded in that concluding line. Whatever Jean Verdenal came to mean to him, it must have been something far beyond what the sparse facts alone may yield. We might come to see that *The Waste Land* represented Eliot's almost overwhelming effort to bring about an imaginative transfiguration of those facts, to find his way by whatever tortuous path to the innocence that he knew instinctively lay at the center of his feelings for Jean Verdenal.

Another of Eliot's literary enthusiasms may be helpful biographically. Djuna Barnes' *Nightwood* (1937) is the most interesting work of a writer who occupies a small niche in American literary history, and mention of this novel is almost invariably accompanied by a quotation praising it by T.S. Eliot. Eliot wrote an Introduction for the novel in 1937, and his extravagant praise often leads to puzzlement in the novel's readers, who search in it some measure of what he apparently found.[19] In his Introduction, he affirms that he read the novel many times, and even so it took some time for him to come to an "appreciation of its meaning as a whole." In working his way to a summary of that meaning, Eliot reveals his fascination with Dr. Matthew O'Connor, a leading character who turns out to be a transvestite. The one passage that Eliot examines in his remarks is the sensational chapter in which a female character inadvertently enters the doctor's room, finding him in bed in female clothes and wig, surrounded by a jumble of female underclothes and finery. Eliot comments that the doctor is the character that gives "the book its vitality," and he insists that the novel is "not a psychopathic study" (a label often applied to it in the handbooks).

Eliot then writes what we may take to be his view of the book's "meaning as a whole": "The miseries that people suffer through their particular abnormalities of temperament are visible on the surface: the deeper design is that of the human misery and bondage which is universal. In normal lives this misery is mostly concealed; often, what is most wretched of all, concealed from the sufferer more effectively than from the observer. The sick man does not know what is wrong with him: he partly wants to know, and mostly wants to conceal the knowledge from himself." The language here seems to hover on the verge of revelation, and we recognize it as the language that Eliot came to apply to his own experience at the time in 1921 he retreated to Lausanne, with his "emotional derangement," producing the poem that became in effect the exorcising of a demon. But though Eliot offers no revelations, he does turn suddenly autobiographical: "In the Puritan morality that I remember, it was tacitly assumed that if one was thrifty, enterprising, intelligent, practical and prudent in not violating social conventions, one ought to have a happy and 'successful' life. Failure was due to some weakness or perversity peculiar to the individual; but the decent man need have no nightmares." Nowadays, Eliot continues, the blame is placed with society, but this is little different from the Puritan belief: "It seems to me that all of us, so far as we attach ourselves to created objects and surrender our wills to temporal ends, are eaten by the same worm." This, Eliot concludes, is the "profounder significance" of *Nightwood,* making it impossible, unless we "harden our hearts in an inveterate sin of pride," to dismiss the novel as a "horrid sideshow of freaks."

Eliot's meaning tends at times in this passage to turn opaque, but he seems to be saying that, inasmuch as we are all "eaten by the same worm," we can all, at some level, in some measure, identify with the bizarre characters of *Nightwood.* As a matter of fact, Dr. Matthew O'Connor may have reminded Eliot of a figure in one of his early poems, still unpublished in 1937, "The Death of Saint Narcissus." The poem is a sympathetic treatment of an invert who "could not live mens' ways," and some of its opening lines ended up in Part I of *The Waste Land* (the poem appears among the *Waste Land* manuscripts published in 1971).[20] In my analysis of the poem (Chapter 5), I explore the possible links of this poem with Jean Verdenal.

4

Critical Theory

Escaping Personality— Exorcising Demons

In words, like weeds, I'll wrap me o'er,
　　Like coarsest clothes against the cold:
　　But that large grief which these enfold
Is given in outline and no more.
　　　　　　　Alfred, Lord Tennyson

Although Eliot's letters are not now available for whatever they
might be able to contribute to the conjectures here set forward, he
did leave in public view a large body of criticism that takes on new
dimensions of meaning when placed in a biographical frame. Eliot's
criticism has, of course, had great impact on the major critical move-
ments of the twentieth century, giving them some of their most
important ideas and ingenious terms. I should emphasize that to attempt to see that criticism biographically is not to attempt to diminish its significance in the evolution of contemporary critical theory.

But Eliot himself came, in his later career, to disparage, if not
repudiate, his early theoretical criticism. In "The Frontiers of Criticism" (1956) he wrote: "The best of my *literary* criticism—apart from
a few notorious phrases which have had a truly embarrassing success
in the world—consists of essays on poets and poetic dramatists who
had influenced me."[1] Those "notorious phrases" that Eliot so casually refers to ("objective correlative," "dissociation of sensibility")

formed, of course, a substantial part of the basis for the modern critical revolution that came to be called the "New Criticism."

That Eliot was serious in his disparaging references to his early criticism is confirmed by his more elaborate comments in "To Criticize the Critic" (1961). He notes with some bemusement that "an essay called *Tradition and the Individual Talent* . . . still enjoys immense popularity among those editors who prepare anthological text-books for American college students."[2] It is precisely such theoretical essays among his work, he goes on to say, that have "least chance of retaining some value for future readers"; his essays on individual poets, he believes, will remain interesting for those who read his poetry.

But what, he asks, of the "generalizations, and the phrases which have flourished, such as 'dissociation of sensibility' and 'objective correlative'"? His answer is not reassuring to those who have built their critical systems on these concepts: "I am not sure, at this distance of time, how valid are the two phrases I have just cited: I am always at a loss what to say, when earnest scholars, or schoolchildren, write to ask me for an explanation." What follows is a kind of confession that the terms had long since ceased to serve their author, and that he could summon no faith in their durability: the terms, he says, "have been useful in their time. They have been accepted, they have been rejected, they may soon go out of fashion completely: but they have served their turn as stimuli to the critical thinking of others." But if, Eliot predicts, these terms are remembered a century hence, "it will be only in their historical context, by scholars interested in the mind" of his generation.[3]

In short, the older Eliot himself began to see his earlier criticism in a historical-biographical context, and, by implication, seemed to invite his readers to approach it in that way. I would like to look briefly at possible connections between Eliot's critical pronouncements made during three periods of his life when he was undergoing, to some degree, psychic stress: the time leading up to his hospitalization at Lausanne in late 1921; the time he had his solicitors arrange a permanent separation from Vivienne in 1932–33; and the time he ordered his solicitors to suppress the John Peter "new" reading of *The Waste Land* in 1952. It goes without saying, of course, that I shall not attempt to assess the validity of critical positions, but will focus on their possible biographical derivations.

"Emotional Derangement" Leading to Lausanne, 1921

During this early period of his career, Eliot made some of his most influential statements about the gulf that should separate personally felt emotion and the emotions evoked by poetry, formulating such doctrines as the "impersonal theory of poetry" and the "objective correlative." So strongly formulated were these doctrines, and so often repeated in published form as to seem obsessional, it comes as something of a surprise to discover that privately Eliot seemed to be planning his own poetry (and particularly *The Waste Land*) from his own personal experience and feelings.

In the 1971 edition of the *Waste Land* manuscripts, Valerie Eliot provided an "Introduction" in the form of a chronology, meticulously reconstructing (but with precise selection) Eliot's life as it led up to the publication of *The Waste Land*. In the process, she quoted from and paraphrased unpublished letters that appear to substantiate much of our speculation about Eliot's biography. Most interesting, perhaps, is a January 1916 letter to Conrad Aiken. It is useful to recall that Jean Verdenal had been killed in early 1915, that Eliot had married suddenly in June 1915, that in January 1916 (the time of Eliot's letter to Aiken) Bertrand Russell had taken Eliot's wife off alone on a seaside holiday at Torquay. All of these data provide a necessary backdrop to Aiken's letter, as summarized by Valerie Eliot. She writes: "His wife had been very ill, he [Eliot] told Aiken on the 10th [of January 1916]; his friend Jean Verdenal had been killed . . . and he had been so 'taken up with the worries of finance and Vivien's health' that he had 'written nothing lately. I *hope* to write when I have more detachment. But I am having a wonderful time nevertheless. I have *lived* through material for a score of long poems in the last six months. An entirely different life from that I looked forward to two years ago. Cambridge seems to me a dull nightmare now.' "[4]

In the unpublished letters of this period quoted by Valerie Eliot, a recurring theme is that the creative stream has run dry but that *personal* experiences are accumulating that will provide the material for later poems. Eliot wrote to his brother, Henry, 6 September 1916: "I often feel that J. A[lfred] P[rufrock] is a swan-song, but I never mention the fact because Vivien is so exceedingly anxious that I shall equal it, and would be bitterly disappointed if I do not. . . . The present year has been, in some respects, the most awful nightmare of anxiety that the mind of man could conceive, but at least it is not dull, and it has its compensations." In late 1917 (23 December 1917), Eliot wrote to his father: " . . . everyone's individual lives are so swallowed up in the one great tragedy that one almost ceases to have personal experiences or emotions, and such as one has seem so unimportant, where before it would have seemed interesting even to tell about a lunch of bread and cheese. It's only very dull people who feel they have more in their lives now—other people have too much. I have a lot of things to write about if the time ever comes when people will attend to them."[5]

In this same year, 1917, when Eliot seemed to be saying in his letters that he was accumulating personal experiences for use in his poetry, he wrote "Tradition and the Individual Talent," in which he elaborated in what appear to be obsessional ways his "impersonal theory of poetry." A few sentences extracted from this overly familiar essay will indicate what I mean by "obsessional": "The progress of an artist is a continual self-sacrifice, a continual extinction of personality"; "The business of the poet is not to find new emotions, but to use the ordinary ones and, in working them up into poetry, to express feelings which are not in actual emotions at all"; "Poetry is not a turning loose of emotion, but an escape from emotion; it is not the expression of personality, but an escape from personality. But, of course, only those who have personality and emotions know what it means to want to escape from these things."[6] *Want to escape!* Such language seems not shaped by the "impersonal theory" but by a personal anguish (and the possible need for concealment) that lies behind the theory itself. Only a few years after formulation of his "impersonal theory of poetry," Eliot would confess to Richard Aldington that he suffered from an "emotional derangement which has been a lifelong affliction" (see Chapter 3).

It is not necessary to disentangle completely the personal feelings that shaped the "impersonal theory of poetry" to assume that Eliot was addressing primarily himself, placing off-limits *his* personal experiences, *his* private feelings for direct use in poetry, and searching about for the method or formula whereby these experiences and feelings could be used indirectly, obliquely, and thus *escaped from* (or sublimated). By the time he wrote his essay "On Hamlet and His Problems" (1919), his formulation of the theory had become more precise, if at the same time rather rigid: "The only way of expressing emotion in the form of art is by finding an 'objective correlative'; in other words, a set of objects, a situation, a chain of events which shall be the formula of that *particular* emotion; such that when the external facts, which must terminate in sensory experience, are given, the emotion is immediately evoked."[7] In 1919, of course, *The Waste Land* was three years away, but Eliot was already beginning to work on parts of it. His later remarks about its composition (such as "I wasn't even bothering whether I understood what I was saying"—see Chapter 2) are at radical variance with the theories he was propounding publicly about the nature of poetry.

In 1921, in "The Metaphysical Poets," Eliot explained his view of what went wrong with poetry, historically, through formulation of his well-known theory of the "dissociation of sensibility" (the separation of feelings from the "ratiocinative") in poetry after the Metaphysical Poets of the seventeenth century. And in his formulation of this theory, Eliot sketched this view of the ideal poet, with a sensibility not "dissociated" but integrated and intact: "When a poet's mind is perfectly equipped for its work, it is constantly amalgamating disparate experiences; the ordinary man's experience is chaotic, irregular, fragmentary. The latter falls in love, or reads Spinoza, and these two experiences have nothing to do with each other, or with the noise of the typewriter or the smell of cooking; in the mind of the poet these experiences are always forming new wholes."[8] New wholes, perhaps, like *The Waste Land,* which Eliot might well have thought he had been constructing along the lines he described here. What the passage reveals is that Eliot's long poem did indeed contain (was constructed out of) biography—but a submerged biography, a combining of disparate experiences that somehow concealed the original experiences at the same time it absorbed them.

When, in his Preface to the 1928 edition of *The Sacred Wood* (which had collected his essays originally in 1920), Eliot reconsidered his earlier critical statements, he found himself already beyond his former positions: " . . . especially I detect frequently a stiffness and an assumption of pontifical solemnity which may be tiresome to

many readers." The little Preface is a major disclaimer, and displays
a growing dissolution of certitude about (but continuing fascination
with) the relation of biography to poetry: "But we observe that we
cannot define even the technique of verse; we cannot say at what
point 'technique' begins or where it ends; and if we add to it a
'technique of feeling,' that glib phrase will carry us but little farther.
We can only say that a poem, in some sense, has its own life; that its
parts form something quite different from a body of neatly ordered
biographical data; that the feeling, or emotion, or vision, resulting
from the poem is something different from the feeling or emotion
or vision in the mind of the poet."[9] With *The Waste Land* now some
six years behind him, and with the variety of reactions and readings
that poem inspired, Eliot remains puzzled with the relation of experience and poetry. He seems to be saying here that in formulating
out of his own disparate experiences a new whole that became *The
Waste Land,* he perhaps knew what new emotion or vision he was
striving to evoke, but that none of the readers of the poem felt
it—they did not perceive "the feeling or emotion or vision in the
mind of the poet." In short, the passage above seems written out of
Eliot's perhaps unsettling experience that *The Waste Land* did indeed
have "its own life"—not the personal life of Eliot which was deliberately fragmented, and not the life that Eliot planned out of the
disparate materials of his own experiences, but a life that its readers
brought to it that Eliot had not conceived or imagined.

Separation from Vivienne, 1932–33

There can be little doubt that Eliot's separation from Vivienne in the
early thirties was one of the traumatic events of his life. He could not
arrange the separation himself, nor could he confront Vivienne as it
was being arranged. He went off to lecture at Harvard during 1932–
33, and in his absence his solicitors followed his orders in arranging
the separation in such a way that Eliot would not have to face his
wife of some eighteen years again. It should not be surprising that it
was shortly after the separation that Eliot remembered so vividly, in

his "Commentary" in *The Criterion,* his youthtime associate, Jean Verdenal—"a sentimental sunset," the Luxembourg Gardens, a "branch of lilac." It should not be surprising, either, that during this period of stress Eliot's thoughts would go back to the writing of that poem in which he had somehow embedded his feelings about his dead friend and his estranged wife.

The major Eliot commentary from this period is the book based on his Harvard lectures, *The Use of Poetry and the Use of Criticism* (1933) and its closing pages are filled with references to the earlier period of Eliot's life, and particularly to *The Waste Land.* The subject comes up first in Eliot's observations about I.A. Richards' comments on *The Waste Land.* Richards' comments that attract Eliot's attention are, in fact, somewhat offhand, appearing in a listing he is making of the jobs of work a critic must perform to understand *The Waste Land* (reading Jessie Weston, figuring out Tiresias). From the list, Eliot seizes only one, and his choice is perhaps telling. After remarking that Richards is "very acute," Eliot continues: "But he observes that Canto XXVI of the *Purgatorio* illuminates my 'persistent concern with sex, the problem of our generation, as religion was the problem of the last.' I readily admit the importance of Canto XXVI, and it was shrewd of Mr. Richards to notice it; but in his contrast of sex and religion he makes a distinction which is too subtle for me to grasp" (pp.126–27).

What was shrewd of Mr. Richards to notice was the relevance to *The Waste Land* of Canto XXVI of the *Purgatorio*—that is, the canto of "The Lustful," portraying the straying bands of sodomites and other devotees of lust, with one of whom, Arnaut Daniel, the poet of *The Waste Land* identifies directly in the closing lines of the poem. The relation of this canto to *The Waste Land* will be dealt with in the analysis in later chapters. It is sufficient here to note that Eliot seems to be pointing, in calling attention to Richards' offhand comment, to a central aspect of *The Waste Land* that its commentators up to that time had overlooked. And there is the phrase that seems to be left dangling, both by Richards and Eliot—"the persistent concern with sex, the problem of our generation."[10]

Not many pages beyond this passage in *The Use of Poetry and the Use of Criticism,* Eliot's thoughts appear to stray back to his experience in writing his early long poem. The language he uses is about as far from the language used in formulating the "objective correlative" as it is possible to get:

> I know, for instance, that some forms of ill-health, debility or anaemia, may (if other circumstances are favourable) produce an efflux of poetry in a way approaching the condition of automatic writing—though, in contrast to the claims sometimes made for the latter, the material has obviously been incubating within the poet, and cannot be suspected of being a present from a friendly or impertinent demon. What one writes in this way may succeed in standing the examination of a more normal state of mind; it gives me the impression, as I have just said, of having undergone a long incubation, though we do not know until the shell breaks what kind of egg we have been sitting on. To me it seems that at these moments, which are characterised by the sudden lifting of the burden of anxiety and fear which presses upon our daily life so steadily that we are unaware of it, what happens is something *negative*: that is to say, not "inspiration" as we commonly think of it, but the breaking down of strong habitual barriers—which tend to re-form very quickly. Some obstruction is momentarily whisked away. The accompanying feeling is less like what we know as positive pleasure, than a sudden relief from an intolerable burden. (Pp. 144–45)

A little later in this same essay, Eliot adds in what seems almost an aside: "I am not even sure that the poetry which I have written in this way is the best that I have written; and so far as I know, no critic has ever identified the passages I have in mind" (p. 146).

We now know, of course, that Eliot had *The Waste Land* in mind here, and particularly Part V written at Lausanne. And it is of special interest to observe in a passage only a few lines on beyond this reference to *The Waste Land*, that Eliot, wrestling with the mystery of the way images become charged with emotion, describes images that sink to the "depths of . . . feeling" and are "saturated, transformed there—'those are pearls that were his eyes'—and brought up into daylight again." This line from Ariel's song in *The Tempest* turns out to be (as readers of *The Waste Land* know) a kind of refrain sounding or subliminally suggested throughout *The Waste Land* (see analysis below), and is intimately connected with Phlebas the Phoenician, the drowned sailor, of Part IV.

"Those are pearls that were his eyes": perhaps it is this line, surfacing momentarily to consciousness in 1933, that sets Eliot off on a series of enigmatic memories, in speculation about the mystery of the emotional meaning of images: "Why, for all of us, out of all that we have heard, seen, felt, in a lifetime, do certain images recur, charged with emotion, rather than others? The song of one bird, the leap of one fish, at a particular place and time, the scent of one flower, an old woman on a German mountain path, six ruffians seen through an open window playing cards at night at a small French railway junction where there was a watermill: such memories have symbolic value, but of what we cannot tell, for they come to represent the depths of feeling into which we cannot peer. We might just as well ask why, when we try to recall visually some period in the past, we find in our memory just the few meagre arbitrarily chosen set of snapshots that we do find there, the faded poor souvenirs of passionate moments" (p. 148).

The lyric quality of this passage, coming as it does in the context we have noted, at a time of particular personal stress in Eliot's marriage, conjures a vision almost of life lost—lost in the past. The images Eliot conjures here as examples go all the way back to his youth in Paris and Germany, the youth he remembers (as we have seen) through the romantic haze of his relationship with Jean Verdenal. Given all the links of association and the implications and suggestiveness, we might reasonably assume that for Eliot the line from Ariel's song—"Those are pearls that were his eyes"—was connected profoundly in the depths of his feeling with the devastating death of Jean Verdenal in 1915.

Legal Suppression of the "New" Reading of The Waste Land, *1952*

Although Eliot's biographers have not dealt with John Peter's 1952 essay interpreting *The Waste Land* as a nightmarish vision of a consciousness that is suffering from the devastating loss of an intimate friend, it seems clear from Peter's report of Eliot's reaction, both legally and emotionally, that the entire affair made considerable impact on Eliot and affected measurably the way he talked about literature in his later lectures, including the veiled references he made to his own early poetry. Eliot's theory of poetry during his late years was radically different from his "impersonal theory of poetry" and the doctrine of the "objective correlative" of his early career. There are no doubt numerous causes for the shift in Eliot's view, but we may well see the threat of the Peter essay as a primary motive in his sorting through his beliefs once again and putting them systematically on record. The most revealing essays in this regard are "The Three Voices of Poetry" (1953) and "The Frontiers of Criticism" (1956).

We have already seen that at an earlier time Eliot had begun to talk about the relation of poetry to illness, as discussed above in a key passage from the 1933 lectures, *The Use of Poetry and the Use of Criticism* (see also Valerie Eliot's footnote 1, page 71, in the *Waste Land* manuscripts, in which Eliot confesses that he was describing his own experience in writing his long poem when he linked poetry and illness in his 1931 essay "The Pensées of Pascal"). But it was not until he wrote "The Three Voices of Poetry" that he gave an emphatic endorsement to illness as a primary source for poetry in a full-scale discussion. The language Eliot uses seems agitated beyond the needs of any visible cause, and in its extremity resembles in some respects the extremities of language he used in his 1917 essay "Tradition and the Individual Talent," though the positions appear diametrically opposed. We might well relate the agitation to unrevealed biographical events, in the earlier instance Eliot unconsciously trying to create a theory to justify his exorcism of pain and grief over the loss of Jean Verdenal through indirect (that is, impersonal) expression of it, and in the later instance Eliot unconsciously trying to explain the writing of *The Waste Land* to himself and (in some obscure sense) to John Peter—as an act of therapy and exorcism. Though at first glance Eliot's two positions might appear to be opposed—as impersonal is to personal—a deeper look reveals that in fact there is continuity between the younger Eliot calling for a poetic process in which there is "escape from" personality and the older Eliot describing a poetic process in which the "extinction" and "escape," or something very like them, take place.

In "The Three Voices of Poetry," written the year following the affair of the Peter essay, Eliot defined the "first voice" as that of the poet talking to himself, or to no one; and in Eliot's description of it, it seemed always a poetry that originated in torment and that was expelled with relief. It is impossible to read the following passage, keeping in mind the various references Eliot made to the composition of *The Waste Land* discussed in Chapter 2 above, without realizing that he is describing in detail the way he wrote his own famous long poem:

> In a poem which is neither didactic nor narrative, and not animated by any other social purpose, the poet may be concerned solely with expressing in verse—using all his resources of words, with their history, their connotations, their music—this obscure impulse [an "embryo" which is "nothing so definite as an emotion" and "more certainly not an idea"]. He does not know what he has to say until he has said it, and in the effort to say it he is not concerned, at this stage, with other people at all: only with finding the right words or, anyhow, the least wrong words. He is not concerned whether anybody else will ever listen to them or not, or whether anybody else will ever understand them if he does. He is oppressed by a burden which he must bring to birth in order to obtain relief. Or, to change the figure of speech, he is haunted by a demon, a demon against which he feels powerless, because in its first manifestation it has no face, no name, nothing; and the words, the poem he makes, are a kind of form of exorcism of this demon. In other words again, he is going to all that trouble, not in order to communicate with anyone, but to gain relief from acute discomfort; and when the words are finally arranged in the right way—or in what he comes to accept as the best arrangement he can find—he may experience a moment of exhaustion, of appeasement, of absolution, and of something very near annihilation, which is in itself indescribable. And then he can say to the poem: "Go away! Find a place for yourself in a book—and don't expect *me* to take any further interest in you."[11]

"He does not know what he has to say until he has said it. . . . " In his 1959 *Paris Review* interview, Eliot said of *The Waste Land:* "I wasn't even bothering whether I understood what I was saying."¹² Eliot's language in the passage above, when connected with the biographical context we have constructed for the writing of *The Waste Land,* takes on a resonance far more personal than theoretical: "oppressed by a burden," "haunted by a demon," "exorcism of this demon," "relief from acute discomfort," "a moment of exhaustion, of appeasement, of absolution, and of something very near annihilation." Creativity as sublimation? Poetry as therapy? We are very close to some such notion, but Eliot seems in this passage less interested in abstract theory than in laying some old psychic ghosts to rest, exorcising once again memories that the Peter article has painfully recalled.

Almost as though he had the John Peter essay directly in mind, Eliot begins his very next paragraph after the quote above: "I don't believe that the relation of a poem to its origin is capable of being more clearly traced. . . . But if, either on the basis of what poets try to tell you, or by biographical research, with or without the tools of the psychologist, you attempt to explain a poem, you will probably be getting further and further away from the poem without arriving at any other destination. To attempt to explain the poem by tracing it back to its origins will distract attention from the poem, to direct it on to something else which, in the form in which it can be apprehended by the critic and his readers, has no relation to the poem and throws no light upon it."¹³ Assuming for the moment that Eliot has John Peter on *The Waste Land* in mind here, we might note that the poet does not deny that the critic traced the poem back to its origins; but the origins distracted attention to something other than the poem—that is, we may assume, the poet's biographical experience with Jean Verdenal. But this experience, Eliot says (if we are reading him right), cannot throw light upon the poem—*in the form in which it can be apprehended by the critic and his readers.* In other words, to condense swiftly a lot of conjecture, if critic and readers could apprehend the Eliot-Verdenal experience as Eliot himself apprehends or apprehended it, then it might, Eliot implies, throw light on *The Waste Land.*

Another example of what appears to be Eliot's sensitivity to the John Peter essay is worth noting. In "The Frontiers of Criticism"

(1956), he writes: "Perhaps the form of criticism in which the danger of excessive reliance upon causal explanation is greatest is the critical biography, especially when the biographer supplements his knowledge of external facts with psychological conjectures about inner experience. I do not suggest that the personality and the private life of a dead poet constitute sacred ground on which the psychologist must not tread. The scientist must be at liberty to study such material as his curiosity leads him to investigate—so long as the victim is dead and the laws of libel cannot be invoked to stop him."[14] It is hard to imagine that Eliot wrote about the "laws of libel" without wincing in memory of the John Peter article. And he goes on for some paragraphs worrying the problem of biography and criticism in such a gingerly way as to suggest his own inner agitation. For example: "Nor is there any reason why biographies of an author should not be written. Furthermore, the biographer of an author should possess some critical ability; he should be a man of taste and judgment, appreciative of the work of the man whose biography he undertakes. And on the other hand any critic seriously concerned with a man's work should be expected to know something about the man's life. But a critical biography of a writer is a delicate task in itself; and the critic or the biographer who, without being a trained and practicing psychologist, brings to bear on his subject such analytical skill as he has acquired by reading books written by psychologists, may confuse the issues still further." John Peter on *The Waste Land* again? It is well known that Eliot specified that his papers not be made available for a biography—not even if a biographer appeared who was both a trained and practicing psychologist. Come to think of it, can anyone recall a recognized literary critic who is? Eliot seems to have set up impossible conditions, and then in his own case refused to bow even to them.

Our views of Eliot's literary theories seem on the verge of fulfilling Randall Jarrell's uncanny predictions about Eliot in 1963, when he wrote in "Fifty Years of American Poetry": "Won't the future say to us in helpless astonishment: 'But did you actually believe that all those things about objective correlatives, classicism, the tradition, applied to *his* poetry? Surely you must have seen that he was one of the most subjective and daemonic poets who ever lived, the victim and helpless beneficiary of his own inexorable compulsions, obsessions? From a psychoanalytical point of view he was far and away the most interesting poet of your century. But for you, of course, after the first few years, his poetry existed undersea, thousands of feet below that deluge of exegesis, explication, source listing, scholarship, and criticism that overwhelmed it. And yet how bravely and personally it survived, its eyes neither coral nor mother-of-pearl but plainly human, full of anguish!' "[15] In effect, Randall Jarrell seems to have seen and understood intuitively what later publications and revelations have tended to confirm.

5

A Suppressed "Ode"
Confessional Poem

And this, O this shall henceforth be the token of comrades, this
   calamus-root shall,
Interchange it youths with each other! let none render it back!
                                                    Walt Whitman

One of the most intriguing poems Eliot ever wrote, "Ode," was published in *Ara Vos Prec,* a special 1920 volume of poems published in England with a printing of only 264 copies. The title of this volume has some relevance to "Ode" in particular. The Provençal phrase comes from Arnaut Daniel's speech at the end of Canto XXVI of Dante's *Purgatorio;* in Canto XXVI ("The Rein of Lust"), Dante encounters the souls of the Sodomites and the souls of the Lustful. One of these, Arnaut Daniel, a twelfth-century troubadour from Provence, emerges briefly to speak with Dante and Virgil, fellow poets, expressing his regrets for his past follies and his hope for the future. And then he speaks the words that Eliot has used frequently (see discussions in Chapters 4, 10, and 11):

> "Ara vos prec, per aquella valor
>   que vos guida al som de l'escalina,
>   sovegna vos a temps de ma color"
> Poi s' ascose nel foco che gli affina.
>   (XXVI, 145–48)

> "I pray you, by that virtue
>   that guides you to the summit of the stair,

> be mindful in your time of my pain."
> Then he dived back into the fire that refines them.

(It is of interest to recall in passing that this volume is the one that carries the Dante epigraph that Eliot was to use later in dedication of the *Prufrock* poems to Jean Verdenal—but without mention of Verdenal.) Of all the poems that appeared in *Ara Vos Prec,* "Ode" presents a "tortured" speaker who seems most clearly identifiable with Arnaut Daniel. But when the American edition of this volume was prepared, the title was changed to *Poems,* the contents were rearranged, and "Ode" was dropped in favor of the prose-poem "Hysteria," a probable portrait of Vivienne. Eliot never again published "Ode."[1]

The only evidence we have as to the date of composition of "Ode" is presented by Donald Gallup in his report of his examination of Eliot manuscripts in the *Times Literary Supplement* (7 November 1968). On the typescript appears: "Ode on Independence Day, July 4th, 1918."[2] I see no reason to doubt this date, even in reading the poem biographically; Eliot's days of being a bridegroom were, of course, in June 1915, but his memory of them might well have endured for the rest of his life, and certainly for the three years up to the composition of the poem. As to further significance of this manuscript title, it is difficult to say. Surely there must have been irony intended in connecting the "Ode" with July 4: the speaker in the poem is obviously anything but independent, trapped as he seems to be in both marriage and memory.

"Ode" has, unlike other Eliot poems, been little analyzed, and has seemed to defy interpretive penetration. I would like to present a reading here as an introduction to Eliot as a confessional poet, and as an entry into the enigmas, and particularly the enigmatic structure, of *The Waste Land.* The title "Ode" is followed by this epigraph from *Coriolanus* (Act IV, Scene 5, 71–72): "To you particularly, and to all the Volscians/ Great hurt and mischief." The text of the poem:

> Tired.
> Subterrene laughter synchronous
> With silence from the sacred wood
> And bubbling of the uninspired
> Mephitic river.

Misunderstood
The accents of the now retired
Profession of the calamus.

Tortured.
When the bridegroom smoothed his hair
There was blood upon the bed.
Morning was already late.
Children singing in the orchard
(Io Hymen, Hymenaee)
Succuba eviscerate.

Tortuous.
By arrangement with Perseus
The fooled resentment of the dragon
Sailing before the wind at dawn
Golden apocalypse. Indignant
At the cheap extinction of his taking-off.
Now lies he there
Tip to tip washed beneath Charles' Wagon.[3]

Although a biographical reading of this poem does not immediately clear up all its difficulties, it does seem to clear up more than any other kind of reading. We might describe the speaker in the poem as a poet who has somehow found his gift of poetic inspiration turned to poison, who has turned away from a misunderstood kind of poetry ("calamus") he wrote in the past and has been unable to find a new poetic voice, and who remains in a state of paralysis caught between the painful reality of a destructive, loveless marriage and the poignant memory of a dead friend, the loss of whose love has left a deep psychic wound of bitterness and anguish. We *might* posit such a speaker, but we know that the outline pretty much fits Eliot's own situation at the time the poem was written. If we come to see the poem as a confessional poem, we then can perhaps understand why Eliot never permitted its republication.

The epigraph of "Ode" comes from Act IV, Scene 5, of *Coriolanus*, a Shakespeare play that Eliot has listed as one of his favorites (in "To Criticize the Critic"), and that he refers to again at a critical juncture near the end of *The Waste Land* in another context suggesting anguish over the loss of a friend—but more about this in Chapter 10. The Coriolanus conjured in the epigraph (compatible with the Coriolanus later dramatized as the supremely proud leader of Eliot's later play fragment, *Coriolan*) has in this scene abandoned Rome and gone over to offer his services to Rome's enemy, and in the speech quoted he is identifying himself:

> My name is Caius Marcius, who hath done
> To thee particularly and to all the Volsces
> Great hurt and mischief. Thereto witness may
> My surname Coriolanus. The painful service,
> The extreme dangers, and the drops of blood
> Shed for my thankless country are requitted
> But with that surname—a good memory
> And witness of the malice and displeasure
> Which thou shouldst bear me.
>
> (Act IV, Scene 5, 69–78)

We might see the speaker of Eliot's poem as one of the victims of the "great hurt and mischief" done by a modern military leader—that is, a leader of World War I of either side responsible for the terrible losses—and in Eliot's case specifically, the loss of Jean Verdenal at the Dardanelles in a battle conceived and planned by modern Coriolanuses.

The body of "Ode" consists of three separate stanzas, each launched by a key word that refers to the speaker's emotional or spiritual state—*Tired, Tortured, Tortuous*—a series of related pains that may be seen as an anatomy of the "great hurt" felt by the speaker as a result of the indiscriminate—but particular—killing of World War I. First of all the speaker is "Tired," and the explanation follows:

> Tired.
> Subterrene laughter synchronous
> With silence from the sacred wood
> And bubbling of the uninspired
> Mephitic river.

The poet finds that, instead of poetic inspiration from the sacred wood, he hears a subterraneous laughter of mockery, and flowing up from the depths not the Pierian spring of the muses but instead the bubbling of the "uninspired" noxious, bad-smelling ("Mephitic") river. In short, the poet has found the usual sources of inspiration either dried up or turned poisonous.

Moreover, even the poetry that he has previously written has not been comprehended:

> Misunderstood
> The accents of the now retired
> Profession of the calamus.

This last is one of the oddest lines of the poem and one of the most cryptic. It might at first glance seem a reference to some kind of strange occupation—or profession. But in the context, "profession" clearly means a declaration or avowal, something considerably beyond a mere "confession," but bearing some resemblance to one. "Profession of the calamus": the reference is unmistakable, and may be the only clear and distinct reference in all of Eliot's poetry to the poetry of Walt Whitman. Eliot's relation to Whitman—a relationship of repulsion-attraction—has been the subject of one small book.[4] But so far as I know, Eliot has not in his scattered critical comments on Whitman made reference to Whitman's "Calamus" poems—a cluster of poems in *Leaves of Grass* that stands next to the cluster entitled "Children of Adam." Just as the "Children of Adam" poems are procreational poems celebrating man-woman relationships, the "Calamus" poems are comradeship poems celebrating man-man relationships, and the celebration emphasizes the deepest kind of attachment and intimacy, under suspicion by the time Eliot wrote "Ode" as suggesting more than the merely spiritual. If we boldly read Eliot's lines in biographical context, we understand him to say that he considers his earlier published work, *Prufrock and Other Observations,* misunderstood. And it was this earlier work that was written in "the accents of the now retired/ Profession of the calamus." The accents are "now retired," perhaps, in the sense that all poetic inspiration has dried up—as indicated in the first lines of the poem.

But in what way did *Prufrock and Other Observations* represent a

"profession of the calamus"? The reader of *Ara Vos Prec* will find the
Prufrock poems conveniently accessible: Eliot positioned "Ode" in
the middle of the volume, to come immediately before them—
something like a lead into them. A careful reading of the volume,
and particularly the two long opening poems—"The Love Song of
J. Alfred Prufrock" and "Portrait of a Lady"—shows a paralysis of
feeling in man-woman relationships, an inability of the speaker to
relate profoundly, especially sexually, with the women he encounters. Although "Prufrock" cannot be dealt with in detail here, it
is worth noting that an early version of the poem carried as a subtitle
"Prufrock among the women," and an epigraph consisting of the last
two lines of the favorite Canto XXVI of *Purgatorio*, the canto repre-
senting the souls of the Sodomites and the souls of the Lustful.[5]
Moreover, although much ink has been spilled identifying the "you"
of Prufrock's "Love Song" as another self of Prufrock, Eliot himself
has insisted that the "you" is a male friend: "As for *The Love Song of
J. Alfred Prufrock* anything I say now must be somewhat conjectural,
as it was written so long ago that my memory may deceive me; but I
am prepared to assert that the 'you' in *The Love Song* is merely some
friend or companion, presumably of the male sex, whom the
speaker is at the moment addressing, and that it has no emotional
content whatever."[6] These remarks were sent in a letter to Kristian
Smidt and appear, undated, in his 1961 book on Eliot. In the comment, Eliot seems at first to offer an illumination, and then to with-
draw it as insignificant. If we take Eliot seriously, and see his remark
in the context of the biographical background I have been sketching—
and then read "Prufrock" with the identity of the "you" throughout
established as a male friend, we can understand the meaning of
Eliot's reference to his own "profession of the calamus." Consider,
for example, the suggestiveness of these lines:

> Smoothed by long fingers,
> Asleep . . . tired . . . or it malingers,
> Stretched on the floor, here beside you and me.

In view of such lines, it is difficult to comprehend that the "you" of
the poem "has no emotional content whatever."
    There is more to be said about "Prufrock," and more about the

poems of the *Ara Vos Prec* volume, especially in the light of Eliot's "calamus" reference, but deeper exploration must await another occasion. It remains to point out the most "Calamus"-like aspect of the book is the dedication to Jean Verdenal (1889–1915), killed in the Dardanelles. The quotation from Dante ("Now you are able to comprehend the quantity of love that warms me toward you,/ When I forget our emptiness/ Treating shades as if they were solid"), which stands mysteriously alone at the front of *Ara Vos Prec*, would not catch up with Verdenal's name in public until 1925 (in *Poems*), but the two had surely been long since firmly linked, calamus-fashion, in Eliot's mind. In declaring himself "misunderstood," Eliot perhaps had in mind that the poems of the *Prufrock* volume were criticized as obscure and unpleasant—and that nobody had connected their sentiment with the revelation in the dedication to Jean Verdenal.

The speaker of "Ode" is, then, "tired," "misunderstood," and, next, in perhaps the description of greatest intensity yet, "tortured":

> Tortured.
> When the bridegroom smoothed his hair
> There was blood upon the bed.
> Morning was already late.
> Children singing in the orchard
> (Io Hymen, Hymenaee)
> Succuba eviscerate.

These are probably the most direct and vivid lines of the poem, and they seem compatible biographically with all we know about the strange and hasty marriage of Eliot and Vivienne Haigh-Wood in 1915. The marriage had clearly very early become a torture for Eliot, and the torture was probably, as suggested in this stanza, in the sexual relationship and the revulsion that Eliot probably felt in consummating or tolerating it. This bridegroom smoothing his hair apparently has no memory of sexual rapture, but only a mind for blood on the bed and the lateness of the hour and his own mussed appearance. In his imagination he conjures up children singing in the orchard a wedding chant. Eliot here may have had two allusions in mind, both relevant to the main direction of his poem. First, there appears in Whitman's *Leaves of Grass,* in the "Children of Adam" cluster just preceding the "Calamus" poems, a short poem entitled "O Hymen! O Hymenee!" It is an expression of intense sexual ecstasy: "O hymen! O hymenee! why do you tantalize me thus?/ O why sting me for a swift moment only?/ Why can you not continue? O why do you now cease?/ Is it because if you continued beyond the swift moment you would soon certainly kill me?" These lines can, of course, have only ironic meaning for the "tortured" bridegroom.

But Eliot may well in addition have had in mind Catullus' wedding chant, "Hymen o Hymenaee," a long poem that, in the later stanzas, reminds the husband that in marriage he must give up his previous relationships, including that "Calamus"-like relationship with a "boy-friend favorite." This individual is addressed directly in some of Catullus' most playful (and suggestive) lines:

> Give nuts to the children, you concubine;
> Long enough you have lived at ease
> And played with nuts like a child. You may
> Now be slave to Talasio.
> Boy-friend favorite, give nuts.[7]

But this happy, carefree, and celebratory song of marriage is imprisoned in parentheses in Eliot's stanza and, whatever its source, probably appears only fleetingly in the tortured bridegroom's mind. The stanza ends: "Succuba eviscerate." This bridegroom sees his bride as a succuba: a female demon who has sexual intercourse with men in their sleep. "Succuba eviscerate": in intercourse, this succubus bride disembowels, or perhaps castrates, deprives the bridegroom of his phallus, turning him into—a sterile fisher-king, prepared to write *The Waste Land.*

Tired, Misunderstood, Tortured—Tortuous. All of the descriptive terms have been passive, until this last, which is mildly, defensively active. Tortuous: twisting, winding, indirect, oblique, obscure. Such tortuousity was perhaps inevitable in a poetry—as described in "Tradition and the Individual Talent"—drawing on private experience but submerging "personal emotion." The last stanza of "Ode" is surely tortuous, presenting more opaque lines than the rest of the poem together:

Tortuous.
By arrangement with Perseus
The fooled resentment of the dragon
Sailing before the wind at dawn.
Golden apocalypse. Indignant
At the cheap extinction of his taking-off.
Now lies he there
Tip to tip washed beneath Charles' Wagon.

The stanza ends, clearly, with a body beneath the waters, as though in prologue to the fate of Phlebas the Phoenician in Part IV of *The Waste Land.* We may assume also psychic identification with Jean Verdenal—and his death in the Dardanelles. But by what tortuous path has this stanza succeeded in depositing him there? A bit of research in mythology handbooks reminds us that Perseus, son of Zeus and Danae, killed the Gorgon Medusa and by using her head could turn to stone any who looked directly at it. Ovid's *Metamorphoses* (one of Eliot's favorite sources for lines and allusions) details over some pages Perseus' other exploits—his defeat of Atlas, his winning of the captive Andromeda by direct conflict with the monster-dragon (he soars down on it as it watches his shadow), and his further battles. Is the dragon's "fooled resentment"—resentment because fooled?—that it watched the shadow rather than the real Perseus? Is Perseus' winning of Andromeda through trickery obscurely referring to Eliot's "winning" of Vivienne through deception— deception that concealed his feeling for Verdenal beneath the declaration of his feeling for Vivienne? Ovid further details the jealousies that arose because of Perseus' winning of Andromeda, and the chaotic fighting that broke out because of the jealousies, and the innocent bystanders that were killed in the brawl that followed. Eliot writes, "Golden apocalypse." Does he have in mind, by tortuous indirection, Ovid's story of the ensuing death of Athis and Lycabas— deep friends of the "Calamus" kind—which constitutes a kind of golden apocalypse:

There was a youngster, Athis, from India,
Whose mother was a river-nymph, Limnaee,
And he was beautiful, with beauty doubled

By the rich robes he wore, the purple mantle
With fringe of gold, and a golden chain adorning
His throat, and a golden circlet holding in
His hair, perfumed with myrrh. At sixteen years
He threw the javelin well, and bent the bow
With even greater skill, and would have bent it
Once more, but Perseus, snatching from the altar
A smoldering brand, used it for club and battered
His face to splintered bones.

          And this was seen
By Lycabas, who loved him, very dearly,
As one boy loves another, and who wept
For Athis, gasping out his life, his features
Fouled in his lifeblood, and he seized the bow
Which Athis once had bent. "You have me to fight,
In having killed this boy: all that you gain
Is hate, not praise!" As the last words were spoken,
The arrow was on its way, but missed, and fastened harmless
In Perseus' robe, and Perseus turned, and swung
The scimitar that once had slain the Gorgon
And now slew Lycabas, who, in the darkness
That swam before his eyes, looked once around
For Athis, and once more lay down beside him
And took this comfort to the world of shadows
That in their death the two were not divided.[8]

If this is Eliot's "golden apocalypse," the route is tortuous indeed. But the passage is in harmony with the entire thrust of "Ode." Athis' golden death is a kind of apocalypse (he is a golden youth adorned in dazzling gold), and the speaker of "Ode" may well instinctively identify in a kind of longing for death with Lycabas and his fate.

If these speculations go off in the right direction on Eliot's tortuous path, there still remains the problem of the identity of Perseus. For Eliot he may well be another hero or military leader like Coriolanus, a representative of the public will who leads his men into battle, to make often meaningless and thankless sacrifices of their lives, as in the case of Athis and Lycabas, devoted to each other in a "Calamus" relationship. There were such leaders in World War I, and they were committed to the disastrous 1915 attempt—involving no doubt both *fooling* and *resentment*—to take the Dardanelles during which Jean Verdenal, perhaps "sailing before the wind at dawn," was lost along with thousands of others.

In any event the memory of the "golden apocalypse" appears to move the speaker's thoughts on to a death that has brought unspeakable anguish:

> Indignant
> At the cheap extinction of his taking-off.

The echo here is from *Macbeth,* Act I, Scene 7:

> Besides, this Duncan
> Hath borne his faculties so meek, hath been
> So clear in his great office, that his virtues
> Will plead like angels, trumpet-tongued against
> The deep damnation of his taking-off. . . .

In contrast with Macbeth's king, whose death will arouse great complaint, the death of Jean Verdenal—coming as it does in an apocalypse or holocaust in which countless men lost their lives in senseless combat—is a "cheap extinction," for which the speaker feels a simply anguished indignation.

The "Ode" closes with the speaker's vision of the body beneath the waters:

> Now lies he there
> Tip to tip washed beneath Charles' Wagon.

Charles' Wagon is another name for what most of us know as the Big Dipper, or Ursa Major, the prominent constellation of the northern hemisphere, fully visible throughout Europe and the area of the Dardanelles. This constellation is known as Charles' Wain or Charles' Wagon, derived from Charlemagne, who had his own ambiguous rendezvous with Constantinople. Though the image of the body beneath the waters is briefly presented at the end of the poem— "tip to tip washed beneath Charles' Wagon"—there is the clear suggestion (as later in the case of Phlebas the Phoenician in *The Waste Land*) of cleansing and purification. The sacrifice of life may have been a "cheap extinction," but the experience itself seems to have offered the speaker the grounds for some kind of imaginative transfiguration, however obscure and tenuous.

Tired, misunderstood, tortured, tortuous: the poet's thoughts move from his current uninspired and unsatisfying work, to his previous work that was not comprehended; from his current repellent marriage, to the memory of a dead friend. The present marriage thus becomes linked to the current pollution of the creative wellspring, while the past friendship becomes linked with the creativity of the past with its "profession of the calamus." It is possible, of course, to read "Ode" without reference to Eliot's biography: the emotional exhaustion it evokes is not uncommon, in some sense is universal (or universally comprehensible). But the poem's density renders it cryptic, especially outside the biographical context. When placed in that context, it achieves greater impact, reveals greater depths. The key words of the poem might be taken as descriptive of Eliot as he approached that period of nervous breakdown that led to the writing of *The Waste Land*. And the central consciousness of the smaller work would reappear in essence in the larger: *tired, misunderstood, tortured, tortuous.*

6

Memory and Desire
"Burial of the Dead"

> . . . an imaginary character . . . who has
> suffered an irreversible loss. . . .
>   John Berryman

In attempting to relate *The Waste Land* to biographical data that
appear to have been used in "Ode," we are simply following Eliot's
own repeated admonitions—that *The Waste Land* was a personal
poem, that it was written out of pressures and intensities which the
poet himself did not fully understand or try fully to comprehend. As
a matter of fact, we could, I believe, read *The Waste Land* in the way I
read it on the following pages without reference to Eliot's biography
at all—by simply concentrating on the consciousness of the "persona" in the poem. In such a case, we would simply invent somebody
like Jean Verdenal and the "calamus" relationship for this persona,
and the meaning of the poem would be essentially the same for
either the biographical or the "persona" (impersonal) reading. We
probably can never know, even when all the biographical data are
available, the role Jean Verdenal played in Eliot's life, particularly
his imaginative or psychic life. There may well have been nothing
visible externally but a close friendship, and there may well have
been nothing "overt" beyond this fellow-feeling or comradeship. But
Eliot's imagination could well have transformed the meager facts
beyond recognition, especially after Verdenal's death. And memory
might well have spun in agony over times and opportunities passed
by. It is, after all, human nature to remember the close associations

of ardent youth in a golden haze. And an imaginative mind can change a chance encounter into cataclysmic experience. Emily Dickinson offers only one case of many in which a transcendent imagination derived a great body of love poetry from the most casual of relationships. Eliot may well have created or intensified in retrospect the feelings he experienced in his youthful association. But this imaginative expansion renders them no less valid, no less anguishing, no less proper as the subject of poetry.

We are able to get some notion of the time of composition of *The Waste Land* if we follow Valerie Eliot's clues in her Introduction to the *Waste Land* manuscripts, in which she makes generous use of unpublished letters. In his January 1916 letter to Conrad Aiken, Eliot said: "I have *lived* through material for a score of long poems in the last six months." He mentioned in a 5 November 1919 letter to John Quinn that he had been wanting to "get started on a poem I have in mind." And he wrote his mother in December 1919 that his New Year's resolution was "to write a long poem" that he had had on his mind "for a long time."[1]

By 9 May 1921, Eliot was writing to Pound that he was "wishful to finish a long poem" which was now "partly on paper."[2] Thus, when Eliot went to Lausanne in late 1921 for treatment of his "nerves" (or "psychological troubles"), we may assume that much of *The Waste Land* was already written. There is no need to review fully the bibliographical evidence here,[3] but the evidence appears to be that the primary production at Lausanne was Part V of *The Waste Land,* written through without need for much revision. The other parts of the poem, however, were written at various times, went through revision, incorporated lines from poems written much earlier, and in general "grew" in such complicated ways that they will be impossible to disentangle. But in addition to finishing Part V and other passages at Lausanne, no doubt Eliot carefully put together all the pieces that he had been developing over at least a two-year period into a completed manuscript that he turned over in December 1921 to Ezra Pound for his suggestions. And, as the published manuscripts make clear, Ezra Pound made radical suggestions, most of which were accepted by Eliot with very little question.

Of course, Pound could not know the very private biographical materials out of which Eliot had created his poem. And if Eliot had used these materials only obliquely in his long poem, Pound in his revisions obscured the poem's origins even more—perhaps beyond recovery, had the manuscripts not survived. There is first the problem of the poem's consciousness, which worried Eliot even as he agreed to Pound's revisions. When he realized that Pound had so cut the poem that the poem's consciousness or persona did not project at all clearly, he suggested that "Gerontion" be used as an introductory section—to indicate that the consciousness of *that* poem lay behind the entire *Waste Land.*[4] But Pound would not hear of the addition of "Gerontion," and Eliot acquiesced.[5]

Eliot's footnotes were in part no doubt added to give back to the poem much of what Pound's revision had taken away. Eliot came to disavow the notes: in "Frontiers of Criticism" (1956), he says that at first he wanted to indicate all of his quotations, "with a view to spiking the guns of critics of my earlier poems who had accused me of plagiarism. Then, when it came to print *The Waste Land* as a little book—for the poem on its first appearance in *The Dial* and in *The Criterion* had no notes whatever—it was discovered that the poem was inconveniently short, so I set to work to expand the notes, in order to provide a few more pages of printed matter, with the result that they became the remarkable exposition of bogus scholarship that is still on view to-day. I have sometimes thought of getting rid of these notes; but now they can never be unstuck. They have had almost greater popularity than the poem itself—anyone who bought my book of poems, and found that the notes to *The Waste Land* were not in it, would demand his money back." After pointing out that the notes did not harm other poets by encouraging them to use notes, Eliot adds: "No, it is not because of my bad example to other poets that I am penitent: it is because my notes stimulated the wrong kind of interest among the seekers of sources. It was just, no doubt, that I should pay my tribute to the work of Miss Jessie Weston; but I regret having sent so many enquirers off on a wild goose chase after Tarot cards and the Holy Grail."[6] There is, clearly, a coy note that creeps into this disavowal of the notes toward the end, suggesting that the secrets of *The Waste Land* remain to be discovered. If the notes "stimulated the wrong kind of interest among the seekers of sources," if chasing after Tarot cards and the Holy Grail led far afield from the poem, what would be the right kind of interest? The very biographical materials that we are now here trying to juggle, to sift, to explore? It is possible that Eliot added the notes to pad out the book to please a publisher. It is also possible that the young Eliot saw the notes as an opportunity to direct critics into harmless chasing after mythical and literary sources and to deflect them from the poem's deepest sources, the poet's biography.

But perhaps Eliot's most compelling motive in adding the notes was to give *The Waste Land* a shape, a form, a structure it had lost in Pound's revision. The only way to do this was to restore some kind of consciousness—a still point of the turning poem—as a focal point, to depart from and return to. Eliot's most influential attempt in this direction was in his footnote on Tiresias, who enters the poem in Part III to observe the typist's seduction scene. Eliot wrote: "Tiresias, although a mere spectator and not indeed a 'character,' is yet the most important personage in the poem, uniting all the rest. Just as the one-eyed merchant, seller of currants, melts into the Phoenician sailor, and the latter is not wholly distinct from Ferdinand Prince of Naples, so all the women are one woman, and the two sexes meet in Tiresias. What Tiresias *sees*, in fact, is the substance of the poem." If Pound would not let Eliot have "Gerontion," then Eliot would elevate Tiresias into the position of the poem's consciousness. He might also have chosen to promote the fisher-king.

If Eliot had left the poem more nearly in the form submitted to Pound, it would be clear that both Tiresias and the fisher-king could be subsumed under a central consciousness—a consciousness quite close to that presented in the discarded "Ode"—Tired, Misunderstood, Tortured, Tortuous. Or to pick up one of Eliot's own terms referring to his psychic state during his withdrawal to Lausanne for treatment—a man suffering "an aboulie [lack of will] and emotional derangement which has been a lifelong affliction."[7] It is some such consciousness as this which can identify in passing with an entire sequence of characters in the poem, including Tiresias and the fisher-king. Pound's and Eliot's revisions might be analogized thus: They succeeded in removing from the poem, or in carefully camouflaging, the primary term of a metaphor, leaving only a series of secondary terms whose relationships were obscured because their primary point of referral had faded almost into oblivion.

To restore the poem's original consciousness is to restore this primary term of the metaphor, accomplished most expeditiously by use of the manuscripts. And to begin this job is to begin with the poem's original title and epigraph. Eliot's first title for the poem was "He Do the Police in Different Voices," a line from Dickens' *Our Mutual Friend* spoken by Betty Higden about the foundling Sloppy, and his ability to read the newspapers to her.[8] There are many aspects of this title worth exploring, but the point to be made here is that it implies that all the voices of the poem are from one dramatic center, one consciousness, perhaps even a fragmented personality that can act many parts but can assume none, that can take on roles publicly created (as in the newspapers), but can find no genuine center of self. It may not be too far-fetched (in assuming a persona here close to that of the poet in "Ode") to detect a reference to the exhaustion of the creative flow and the necessary reliance on quotation and allusion, the making of poetry by doing "the *poets* in different voices." Whatever the case, this original title points inward to a central consciousness, in contrast with the ultimate title, *The Waste Land,* which points outward to a sequence of what might be taken as "objective" scenes, constituting a comment not on the poem's consciousness but on the external world and its decaying civilization.

What is said of the title might well be said in stronger terms of the epigraph. Pound wrote Eliot about the quotation from *Heart of Darkness:* "I doubt if Conrad is weighty enough to stand the citation."[9] Eliot was clearly nervous about letting the epigraph go. He replied: "Do you mean not use the Conrad quote or simply not put Conrad's name to it? It is much the most appropriate I can find, and somewhat elucidative." Pound's reply (". . . who am I to grudge him his laurel crown?") suggests an obtuseness on his part to the meaning of Eliot's long poem. His antipathy to Conrad is not that the quotation is inappropriate, but that Conrad may not be important or impressive enough in name. Slight as it is, we seem to have a glimpse here of Pound's imperviousness to the *sense* in contrast to his concern for the *show* of the poem. We might guess that Pound never caught the basic undercurrents of the original poem, which were once again weakened by the shift in epigraph from Conrad to Petronius' *The Satyricon.*

At the climactic moment in *Heart of Darkness,* as Mr. Kurtz is facing imminent death, Marlow says: "Did he live his life again in every detail of desire, temptation, and surrender during that supreme moment of complete knowledge? He cried in a whisper at some image, at some vision,—he cried out twice, a cry that was no more than a breath: 'The horror! The horror!' " At this point in Conrad's fiction, Kurtz appears to achieve his most intense self-revelation. In reliving the moments of his "desire, temptation, and surrender," he evokes an inner vision that impels him to cry out, "The horror! The horror!" In short, his revulsion erupts from insight into the self, his own complicity, not some sweeping vision of contemporary civilization. Moreover, the memory of his life that comes at the moment of his death returns to those elements that will gather resonance throughout *The Waste Land,* as in the opening ("mixing/ Memory and desire") and the closing lines ("The awful daring of a moment's surrender")—elements which embody that biographical dimension under review here. Eliot was right: the Conrad epigraph was "elucidative." In dropping the Conrad and using a Latin-Greek epigraph from the *Satyricon,* Eliot may have satisfied Pound's desire for a more impressive show of learning, but at the same time he lost in diffuseness a certain sharpness of meaning. The speaker in the *Satyricon* quotation says: "With my own eyes I saw the Sibyl of Cumae hanging in a bottle; and when the boys said to her: 'Sibyl, what do you want?' she replied, 'I want to die.' " Here attention is deflected from interior to exterior vision and from contemporary to ancient image, as well as from human to mythic creatures. For Eliot's original meaning, the Cumaean sybil's death wish (she forgot to ask for eternal youth when she got her hundred years of longevity from Apollo) is considerably less suggestive than Kurtz's moral self-realization expressed in "The horror! The horror!"

In suggesting the printing of "Gerontion" as a prelude to the Pound-cut version of his poem, Eliot was feeling the loss of some opening lines that establish the poem's consciousness. In the manuscript version of the poem, there appears a fifty-four-line narrative section that is remarkably accessible for any reader, and that is astonishingly autobiographical, as Valerie Eliot's notes point out. The scene is the Boston of Eliot's Harvard days; specific places (Opera Exchange) are named and specific songs ("By the Watermelon Vine," "The Cubanola Glide") of the period are quoted. The lines present an account of a night of aimless dissipation out on the town by a gang of young men, encompassing a show, drinking at various bars, and scandalous individual adventures (with one member later reporting his unsuccessful attempt to get a woman at "Myrtle's place"), a near arrest for "committing a nuisance," and general behavior that might have been described at the time as hell-raising or deviltry, all very gentlemanly and not terribly depraved. The speaker is one of the group who remains anonymous behind the "we" until near the end of the section, when, as his companions rush off energetically in a sense-less race, he goes off finally by himself. The concluding line: "So I got out [of the cab] to see the sunrise, and walked home." The tone is more one of innocence than anything else, as the debauchery is not all that shocking. Had this section (or a revised version of it) remained at the opening of the poem (and I do not want here to pass judgment on its quality as poetry), it would surely change the way we read what follows. Were we to move from reading the Conrad quotation ("The horror! The horror!") to this section, we would know that we had not yet reached the anguish we might anticipate, but that we were being given a prelude to the loss of innocence and the onset of agony. The speaker of these lines would be established as the consciousness of the poem, Eliot himself—and in this scene the Eliot before the death of Jean Verdenal and the ruinous marriage. Moving from this light-hearted, carefree section to the next lines ("April is the cruellest month"), we encounter a radical new tone in which innocence is re-placed by debilitating experience, and the lighthearted gives way to the anguish.

The next lines in the manuscript constitute the basis for the open-ing lines of the published *Waste Land;* they may take on new mean-ing when we associate them with the original opening of the young Harvard man, after his night out, looking at the sunrise:

> April is the cruellest month, breeding
> Lilacs out of the dead land, mixing
> Memory and desire, stirring
> Dull roots with spring rain.
> Winter kept us warm, covering
> Earth in forgetful snow, feeding
> A little life with dried tubers.
> Summer surprised us, coming over the Königssee

With a shower of rain; we stopped in the colonnade,
And went on in sunlight, into the Hofgarten,
And drank coffee, talking an hour.

Reading the poem to this point, we might guess that it is going to be a poem of unhappy love, love that was fulfilled in the past, but which has tragically ended. The speaker here is carried back to the past by compelling associations, spring rain, lilacs in April. As we have speculated, Eliot himself may have been surreptitiously offering a gloss on this famous passage when his recollection of his student days in Paris was resolved into "the memory of a friend coming across the Luxembourg Gardens in the late afternoon, waving a branch of lilac." The "dull roots" stirred by the spring rain is suggestive of the stirring of the older poet's arrested or paralyzed sexuality. Memory carries him back to that 1910–11 winter in the Paris *pension* with Verdenal ("Winter kept us warm") and the summer trip (if indeed Verdenal accompanied Eliot as I have conjectured) through Europe. Curiously, Eliot changed Königssee, near Berchtesgaden, to Starnbergersee (Wurm lake), near Munich. Possibly Munich's Starnbergersee and Hofgarten are closer to the actual experience: the rain shower and sunlight are all suggestive of happiness and fruition and fulfillment, not only in nature, but personally and creatively: it was in Munich that summer that Eliot completed "The Love Song of J. Alfred Prufrock," a poem in a basic sense about a man who cannot love women.

After these eleven opening lines comes a voice not the poet's, a line of German that translates: "I am no Russian, I come from Lithuania, true German." This is not, I think, one of a medley of mingled voices as sometimes interpreted, but rather a voice that the poet's memory has conjured from the past, that summer in Germany and Munich—in the Hofgarten, maybe, where he (perhaps with Verdenal) met a lady who speaks this line and the others that follow, identifying herself as Marie, as a cousin of the archduke's: "I read, much of the night, and go south in the winter." One diligent scholar, G.K.L. Morris, has discovered what seems to be the source of the Marie passage in *My Past* (1913) by Countess Marie Larisch,[10] but in her footnote to the passage, Valerie Eliot tells us: "The assumption was that Eliot must have read the book, but in fact he had met the author (when and where is not known), and his description of the sledding ["he took me out on a sled,/ And I was frightened"], for example, was taken verbatim from a conversation he had with this niece and confidante of the Austrian Empress Elizabeth."[11] Eliot's widow is the only source for this information, but there seems no reason to doubt it; if the language of the telling is close to the language of the book, it would not be the first time that an author remembered his written words while telling his oral tales. Indeed, if Eliot did pull these words from his own experience, this fact would tend to confirm the intensively personal interpretation we have made of these lines that opened the published *Waste Land*. It is only natural that fateful summer of 1911, in his travels in Germany, the young Eliot would have been attracted to such an elegant, romantic personage, and would even have copied her tale into a notebook to lend atmosphere—give insight into the nature of social Europe—in some work to which he might give birth in the future.

The voice that forcefully enters the poem next sends memory and desire shimmering, fading: "What are the roots that clutch, what branches grow/ Out of this stony rubbish?" This is, surely, the same voice as that of "April is the cruellest month," the voice of the poet of the bleak and barren present, the voice of immediate contemporary reality drowning out the fragile voice of memory. And it is a voice that seems to taunt the poet in the barrenness of his creative faculty:

> Son of man,
> You cannot say, or guess, for you know only
> A heap of broken images, where the sun beats,
> And the dead tree gives no shelter, the cricket no relief,
> And the dry stone no sound of water. Only
> There is shadow under this red rock,
> (Come in under the shadow of this red rock),
> I will show you something different from either
> Your shadow at morning striding behind you
> Or your shadow at evening rising to meet you;
> I will show you fear in a handful of dust.

These lines are some of the most cryptic in *The Waste Land,* and lead immediately into a quotation from Wagner's *Tristan und Isolde* and the passage containing reference to the "hyacinth girl," a subject of intense speculation throughout Eliot criticism. I want to attempt, in a kind of cryptanalytic way, to clear up all the interpretive problems through tracing interconnections between these passages, but by an indirect, even tortuous path that involves still another poem that Eliot left unpublished during his lifetime.

The poem is "The Death of Saint Narcissus," and it has a curious "nonpublication" history, linked with "Prufrock." The poem was submitted to *Poetry* magazine about the same time as "Prufrock" (which was published in *Poetry* in June 1915), and was perhaps written between 1911 and 1915. Valerie Eliot says that Eliot "could not remember when he wrote this poem."[12] Though not published in *Poetry,* it exists in proof in *Poetry*'s files, suggesting that it was withdrawn at a late moment. This "proof" version has been published in *Poems Written in Early Youth* (1967);[13] and what appears to be earlier drafts are included as the first of the miscellaneous poems published with the *Waste Land* manuscripts. "The Death of Saint Narcissus" is one of the most astonishing of Eliot's poems, full of as many ironies as "Prufrock." It is a poem about a narcissistic young man who becomes so entranced by his own physicality and beauty that he wills his way through several transfigurations, a tree, a fish, a young girl. Eliot's imagery in dramatizing these imaginative transformations is reminiscent of some of Whitman's most suggestive and unconventional sexual imagery, and foreshadows some of Dylan Thomas' most daring poems. As a fish—

> With slippery white belly held tight in his own fingers,
> Writhing in his own clutch, his ancient beauty
> Caught fast in the pink tips of his new beauty.

As a young girl—

> Caught in the woods by a drunken old man
> Knowing at the end the taste of his own whiteness
> The horror of his own smoothness,
> And he felt drunken and old.

The autoerotic and homoerotic suggestiveness in these and other lines of "The Death of Saint Narcissus" appear unmistakable. The young man, because "he could not live men's ways," became a "dancer before God" and "danced on the hot sand."

The poem thus ends with the imagery of its beginning, and it is this beginning that must claim our attention as readers of *The Waste Land*:

> Come under the shadow of this gray rock—
> Come in under the shadow of this gray rock,
> And I will show you something different from either
> Your shadow sprawling over the sand at daybreak, or
> Your shadow leaping behind the fire against the red rock:
> I will show you his bloody cloth and limbs
> And the gray shadow on his lips.

The question to be entertained is: what chain of association brought Eliot back to this old, discarded poem, to salvage lines that must have had at one time vivid linkage with the figure of a young, homo-erotic Saint Narcissus? The suggestion I wish to make is clear: the memory of April, lilacs, Paris, Germany, the mixture of "memory and desire," has conjured up a suppressed poem that is connected somehow with those long-ago days. Is it too far-fetched to see "The Death of Saint Narcissus" as a poem distilling (not merely "present-ing") the character of Jean Verdenal, and perhaps written as a com-panion piece to "The Love Song of J. Alfred Prufrock"? Saint Nar-cissus is sympathetically, even tenderly treated in the poem, and suffers from the same malady (only in more intensive form) as does Prufrock—the inability to love women. We might conjecture, then, that Verdenal is Narcissus, Eliot is Prufrock, the two companions of the latter's line, "Let us go, then, you and I" (Eliot claimed that the "you" addressed by Prufrock was a male companion: see discussion in Chapter 5).

The opening lines of "The Death of Saint Narcissus" show the sterile end of Narcissus, his beautiful and intensely feeling and aware body having finally been transfigured into "bloody cloth and limbs" under the gray rock. When the passage is transferred to *The Waste Land*, the images of sterility and death are intensified—with the "dead tree" that "gives no shelter," and the "dry stone no sound of water." But the remarkable suggestion of the earlier passage remains intact in *The Waste Land*—the suggestion of an approaching time when one no longer casts a shadow, when the physical being once so alive fades into substanceless insubstantiality and is resolved into a handful of dust. The striking conception of existing without casting shadows, existing outside the solidity of the flesh, evokes memory of another situation in which one individual momentarily forgot that such bodiless existence was precisely his fate: the quotation from Dante that appeared in the *Ara Vos Prec* volume and that was subsequently attached to the Jean Verdenal dedication of the *Prufrock* poems. Statius in *Purgatorio* addresses Dante's companion Virgil: "Now you are able to comprehend the quantity of love that warms me toward you/ When I forget our emptiness/ Treating shades as if they were solid."

The "Narcissus"-*Waste Land* lines are a vivid reminder to the poem's speaker (or consciousness) of his present state of sterile life without love. And this moment of anguish once again evokes memories of the past, this time via a German quotation from Wagner's opera based on the tragic love story of *Tristan und Isolde:* "The winds blow fresh homeward, my Irish child, where do you tarry?" These lines and their source, surging into consciousness at this point, reinforce the speaker's basic situation in the "shadow of the red rock"— deprived of love through death. But the *Tristan und Isolde* lines lead into some of the poem's most poignant and enigmatic images:

> "You gave me hyacinths first a year ago;
> "They called me the hyacinth girl!"
> —Yet when we came back, late, from the hyacinth garden,
> Your arms full, and your hair wet, I could not
> Speak, and my eyes failed, I was neither
> Living nor dead, and I knew nothing,
> Looking into the heart of light, the silence.

The poet's "memory and desire" have through tortuous paths finally evoked a detailed scene of that past time of happiness and promise that now in his deprivation haunts him. The usual assumption about these lines is that there is a "hyacinth girl" in the speaker's past, but there is little agreement on what the incident evoked by the lines really was or meant. The first thing to note is that the two opening lines of the passage are in quotation marks: it is the poet who gave hyacinths to the speaker of the lines "a year ago," and then they called the speaker "the hyacinth girl." No other references in the passage (or in *The Waste Land*) aid in identifying the speaker of these two lines.

Could the speaker be the original of Saint Narcissus? Emphasis in the key line might be on *girl* (rather than hyacinth): "They called me the hyacinth *girl!*" The meaning thus becomes clearly possible, and is not far removed from Eliot's memory of Jean Verdenal carrying the branch of lilac across Luxembourg Gardens in the Paris of his youth. But there is specific evidence that Eliot wanted the reader to make a masculine association with the hyacinth garden by connecting it with lines associated with the drowned sailor of *The Waste Land* (see discussion a few pages below). Moreover, some interpreters have been puzzled by Eliot's connection of hyacinth with female. As Grover Smith pointed out, the hyacinth is a "sexual symbol," "a male symbol."[14] It is indeed, and surely the story of Hyacinth would have been quite familiar to Eliot. Apollo loved the handsome boy Hyacinthus, and accidentally killed him when the two were throwing the disk. As Ovid relates the story in *Metamorphoses,* Apollo's grief was intense:

> Where is my guilt, except in playing
> With you, in loving you? I cannot die
> For you, or with you either; the law of Fate
> Keeps us apart: it shall not! You will be
> With me forever, and my songs and music
> Will tell of you, and you will be reborn
> As a new flower.[15]

As in the case of Narcissus, who was turned into the flower that bears his name, Hyacinthus became the flower that bears his; and Ovid tells that Apollo made certain that the flower would, in its color and shape, remind the world of the dead boy and lover, and Apollo's grief. Could Eliot have expected none of this myth to have resonance in his poem? But there is also another possible allusion lurking in the hyacinths—to August Strindberg's *The Ghost Sonata* (1907), whose third and final scene is set in the "Hyacinth Room" and dramatizes an abortive (unfulfilled) love scene between "student" and "girl" (the hyacinth girl?), concluding with the death of the girl. One can easily draw connections between the living dead and the exhausted traditions of the world of this play and the world of *The Waste Land*.[16]

What happened in the hyacinth garden, from which the speaker and his friend have returned, late? It seems to me clear that all the language is the language of one who has been transported by ecstasy, by fulfillment of love:

> I could not
> Speak, and my eyes failed, I was neither
> Living nor dead, and I knew nothing,
> Looking into the heart of light, the silence.

The lines bespeak a perfect bliss, beyond speech, beyond sight, neither life nor death, beyond knowledge. Like the traditional mystic, the speaker sees "into the heart of light" to that perfect silence that exists at the still point of the turning world. The passage closest to this experience in *The Waste Land* appears near the end—"The awful daring of a moment's surrender." There all life is transfigured into a new life: "By this, and this only, we have existed." The memory of the fulfillment in the hyacinth garden, which will haunt the poet and the poem, fades with a new pang of loss as another fragment of *Tristan und Isolde* floats into consciousness: "Desolate and empty the sea." This fragment is a reminder of the poet's present aloneness: as in the case of Tristan and Isolde, death has separated the lovers, leaving only anguish and emptiness.

At this point the tone of the poem again changes radically, as Madame Sosostris enters with her "wicked pack of cards." In this passage we seem to be presented the poet's present situation in ironic terms, and we are given what looks like a cast of characters for the poem. Although Madame Sosostris, with her bad cold, seems to be satirized, she also seems to be presenting with her enigmatic cards the cold truth to her visitor, the poet. Eliot in his *Waste Land* footnotes confessed that he did not know the "exact constitution of the Tarot pack of cards," and offered some hints as to the associations he made with certain of the cards turned up. What he seems to suggest is that the meaning of the Tarot cards is not found in the history of the cards, but in their use in the poem—and we might add, in their reference to his own emotionally crucial experiences.

> Here, said she,
> Is your card, the drowned Phoenician Sailor,
> (Those are pearls that were his eyes. Look!)
> Here is Belladonna, the Lady of the Rocks,
> The lady of situations.
> Here is the man with three staves, and here the Wheel

In Eliot's curious footnote, he tells us of these first three cards only that the Phoenician Sailor recurs, and that he arbitrarily identifies the "man with three staves" with the fisher-king (an identification confirmed by these words appearing alongside the passage in the manuscript version).

We may assume, I think, that Madame Sosostris is telling the poet's fortune, and his first and fundamental card is the "drowned Phoenician Sailor," or, in some obscure biographical sense, Jean Verdenal, his dead friend; the second is "Belladonna, the Lady of the Rocks,/ The lady of situations," or, in a similar obscure sense, Vivienne Haigh-Wood, his wife; the third, the "man with three staves," or the poet himself become the fisher-king suffering the sexual wound (loss of Verdenal) that has rendered him impotent in his marriage like the fisher-king of the waste land legend (as described in Jessie Weston's *From Ritual to Romance,* about which more later, especially in Chapter 8). Indeed, these are the cards that fate has dealt the poet at the time of the writing of *The Waste Land,* and thus Madame Sosostris is telling him what he already knows, summarizing his fate that has brought about his sexual-spiritual paralysis. This fate seems summarized by the card of the Wheel—the torture-wheel of endless rounds of boredom of modern suburbia (see discussion of "Death of the Duchess" in Chapter 7). By introducing the fundamental elements of his condition through Madame Sosostris and the Tarot cards, the poet seems to be suggesting that he will "play out" the terms of his predicament in a set of oblique private symbols, he will reenact the critical experiences of his life to discover what he can of the obscure causes of the despair in which he finds himself trapped.

But there remain two other figures from the Madame Sosostris episode:

> And here is the one-eyed merchant, and this card,
> Which is blank, is something he carries on his back,
> Which I am forbidden to see. I do not find
> The Hanged Man. Fear death by water.
> I see crowds of people, walking around in a ring.

If the first figures turned up by the fortune teller reveal the poet's past and present, the next figures murkily predict his future. Eliot himself calls attention in his footnote to the reappearance of the one-eyed merchant—as, indeed, he does reappear in Part III, "The Fire Sermon," where he clearly makes a homosexual proposition, in "demotic French," to the poet, suggesting a "weekend at the Metropole." The fact that the one-eyed merchant turns up in the Tarot pack and that Eliot points out his reappearance in the poem gives him an unusual importance, out of proportion to the space he occupies; think, for example, of the characters who are *not* found in the cards—Stetson, Tiresias, the young man carbuncular, the typist. Clearly the one-eyed merchant symbolizes for the poet one road he might take. Does the one eye, which is not mentioned in the reappearance, suggest limited vision, or physical diminishment—sexual impairment? What does he carry on his back, blank to Madame Sosostris? The weight of a life lived outside the conventional sexual mores of the society? When the merchant reappears, he is unattractive, "Unshaven, with a pocket full of currants," and has business documents at hand, making his unseemly offer of lunch and a weekend clearly in the middle of the distractions of business, perhaps at the tail end of other debaucheries. The burden on his back may be a blank to Madame Sosostris, but it is a revelation—repulsive and terrifying—for the poet.

In his footnotes Eliot provides a gloss for us of the missing card: "The Hanged Man, a member of the traditional pack, fits my purpose in two ways: because he is associated in my mind with the Hanged God of Frazer, and because I associate him with the hooded figure in the passage of the disciples to Emmaus in Part V." All of these somewhat arbitrary associations suggest the sources and the myth itself of Christ's death and resurrection. The absence of this card in Madame Sosostris' deal suggests the poet's future as bleak: perhaps the impossibility of the resurrection of Jean Verdenal, or, more important, the impossibility of the renewal of such an innocent, transfiguring love. The poet must find his way to a reconciliation to his loss—permanent, irreplaceable.

Before leaving this part of *The Waste Land,* we should note a relationship between the hyacinth garden and Phlebas the Phoenician, a connection important to the interpretation explored here. In the first place, the poem juxtaposes the two, with the scene of the hyacinth garden giving way to Madame Sosostris' Tarot cards, the first of which is the "drowned Phoenician Sailor." Immediately after his introduction, we are given a parenthetical line—"(Those are pearls that were his eyes. Look!)"—a line which we take not as Madame Sosostris' but rather her client's (the poet), a line not spoken but meditated. It is surely significant that though Pound marked this line for deletion, Eliot kept it. For the line is, of course, a favorite of Eliot's, and comes from Ariel's song in *The Tempest* (Act I, Scene 2, 396–402):

> Full fadom five thy father lies;
> Of his bones are coral made;
> Those are pearls that were his eyes:
> Nothing of him that doth fade
> But doth suffer a sea-change
> Into something rich and strange.
> Sea nymphs hourly ring his knell. . . .

We have already noted the poignancy with which the haunting line, "Those are pearls that were his eyes," is remembered by Eliot, and have linked the line psychically for Eliot to the death of Jean Verdenal (see Chapters 4 and 9).

And what of the hyacinth garden? The *Waste Land* manuscripts connect it with this recurring Shakespeare line in a revealing passage in Part II, "A Game of Chess." The nervous lady ("lady of situations") of the opening upper-class scene exclaims to what we may well take as her enervated if not impotent husband (the impotent fisher-king of the cards): "Do you know nothing? Do you see noth-

ing? Do you remember/ Nothing?" Her prodding triggers his meditation (not, surely, a spoken reply): "I remember/ The hyacinth
garden. Those are pearls that were his eyes, yes!" It is particularly
noteworthy that it is the "hyacinth garden," not the "hyacinth girl,"
recalled here, reinforcing our conjecture that there is in reality no
such girl in *The Waste Land*. The poet vividly links in his memory the
hyacinth garden and (through the line from *The Tempest*) Phlebas the
Phoenician in a single recollection, which we may in turn connect
with Jean Verdenal. But in the revision of *The Waste Land*, "the
hyacinth garden" was dropped from the line, apparently not on
Pound's but the poet's own decision. The published line reads: "I
remember/ Those are pearls that were his eyes." But then a footnote
to line 126 (apparently meant for the line "Those are pearls that
were his eyes") reads cryptically: "Cf. Part I, l. 37, 48." The curious
reader in following out the references will find line 37: "Yet when
we came back, late, from the Hyacinth garden." And line 48, the
parenthetical meditation of the poet's that follows Madame Sosostris'
first Tarot card, the "drowned Phoenician Sailor": "(Those are
pearls that were his eyes. Look!)." What revision had put asunder
was reconnected in the footnotes. G. Wilson Knight, analyzing this
evidence in his 1972 *Denver Quarterly* essay, reached the inescapable
conclusion: "According to the new text [*The Waste Land: A Facsimile*]
the 'hyacinth girl' appears to be male."[17]

Following Madame Sosostris' fortune telling and prophecies, Part
I of *The Waste Land* presents one final section that brings us into
modern London, but it is a London, as Eliot signals fulsomely in his
footnotes, turned by the agony of the poet into a modern Inferno,
the streets flowing with the living dead, "each man fixed his eyes
before his feet." Pound apparently suggested deletion of the lines

> To where Saint Mary Woolnoth kept the hours
> With a dead sound on the final stroke of nine.

Eliot not only kept the lines, but pointed out in a footnote about the
second line: "A phenomenon which I have often noticed"—this in
reference to the "dead sound on the final stroke of nine." Eliot's
whimsicality here may be taken as his own interest in his poem's
roots in the reality of his own experience. He clearly wanted to

preserve a concrete geography of London, together with realistic detail. We have, moreover, Valerie Eliot's word that Stetson was based on a bank-clerk acquaintance of Eliot.[18] Thus it was *there,* by Saint Mary Woolnoth's, that the poet meets Stetson, and hails him as one who was with the poet "in the ships at Mylae!" The church has faded into a mere detail of geography, keeps the hours with a dead sound, and has no other relevance to the flow of the living dead around it.

The obliqueness of the closing lines spoken by the poet to Stetson need not detain us long, as they have been worried enough in previous interpretive struggles. They are easily harmonized, however, with our reading of the poem. Stetson is one of the crowd, everyman, the reader himself, drawn by the poet into complicity with his own overwhelming sense of doom, anguish, anxiety, guilt. The poet served with Stetson in the ancient sea battles over Mylae (an oblique reference to the World War I sea battles over the Dardanelles, scene of Jean Verdenal's death). Thus, the poet and the reader are ancient companions in pursuit of the world's lusts and desires. Stetson, everyman, you and I—each of us has planted a corpse in his garden—has suppressed his most pleasurable, most anguishing memories down into his deepest feelings—there where it may sprout, blossom, or bloom later in strange ways, in unusual transfigurations:

> "Oh keep the Dog far hence, that's foe to men,
> "Or with his nails he'll dig it up again!
> "You! *hypocrite lecteur!—mon semblable,—mon frère!*"

The Dog of this passage was "foe to man" in the manuscripts but became "friend to man" in revision. Eliot's uncertainty suggests the Dog may well have been neither friend nor foe, but a bit of both. Whatever else the Dog may be (and explicators have proposed every conceivable mythic possibility), he is surely the Dog within, the lust of memory that will not let the past lie buried but digs it up for a psychic confrontation that may be terrifying, paralyzing, even castrating, rendering one impotent as a fisher-king in a waste land. Memory and desire, memory and desire. "Hypocrite reader!—my double,—my brother!" Thus Eliot (borrowing from Charles Baudelaire, as he does not fail to inform us) makes psychic accomplices of us all.

7

In the Cage
"*A Game of Chess*"

This transparent screen fenced out or fenced in, according to the side of the narrow counter on which the human lot was cast. . . .
Henry James

Eliot's original title for Part II of *The Waste Land* was taken from a Henry James novella, "In the Cage." Like the change in the poem's epigraph from Conrad to Petronius, the change in the title of Part II again diffused meaning in deflecting attention from interior feeling to exterior action. "In the Cage" suggests, in a way that "A Game of Chess" does not, the situation of the speaker (the poet) in the opening scene of the section—he is trapped in a loveless marriage, trapped in "memory and desire" that will not let him love a wife he has somehow acquired. Like the female protagonist in the James story, the speaker in *The Waste Land* is imprisoned in a cage from which there is no genuine exit: unable to be a participant in the sexual intrigue that swirls around, he is resigned to being a spectator (as in the second half of "A Game of Chess"). The James story offers many parallels to the Eliot poem that made Eliot's first choice of title a brilliant one: in both story and poem the cage metaphor is appropriate to the animalistic passions dramatized. A young lady working in a telegraph "cage" becomes the center of adulterous maneuvering which she only dimly understands, is fascinated by, and ultimately contributes to. Her social position and the nature of her suitor, Mr. Mudge, are far removed from the "aristocracy" she observes and the glamor she covets. The gap is reproduced in a way in Eliot's "In the

Cage" in the social distance between the opening "society" scene and the closing scene set in a lower-class pub. Moreover, the central affair that the girl "in the cage" observes and assists culminates in a marriage because the lady has acquired some compromising power over the gentleman—thus presenting a situation of the kind we might guess as lying behind the relationship between the woman and the man in the opening scene of Part II of Eliot's poem.

The manuscripts make clear what was not clear to many of the commentators on the published *Waste Land*: that the first half of Part II is a single continuous scene, with the lady introduced at the opening speaking the lines placed in quotation marks that follow, with her husband's meditated (but unspoken) responses sandwiched in without quotation marks. The origin of this scene may be discovered in one of the discarded short poems published with the manuscripts, "The Death of the Duchess."[1] There the scene is set in Hampstead, modern suburbia, where the inhabitants go through their endless and meaningless activities (tea, tennis, "Monday to the city," etc.: "They know what they are to feel and what to think"). When Eliot writes "The inhabitants of Hampstead are bound forever on the wheel," we get a concrete image of what lies behind the Wheel that turned up among the Tarot cards of Madame Sosostris: pointless activity of modern suburban life in the modern city. "The Death of the Duchess" presents what appears to be a loveless marriage, with the husband in the role of speaker:

> What words have we?
>
> I should like to be in a crowd of beaks without words
> But it is terrible to be alone with another person.
>
> We should have marble floors
> And firelight on your hair
> There will be no footsteps up and down the stair.

The speaker, unable to articulate his thoughts, seems emotionally paralyzed:

> My thoughts tonight have tails, but no wings.
> They hang in clusters on the chandelier

Or drop one by one upon the floor.
Under the brush her hair
Spread out in little fiery points of will
Glowed into words, then was suddenly still.

Many of these lines and images survive in *The Waste Land*. In "The Death of the Duchess," the woman is given lines from *The Duchess of Malfi* which do not survive the revision. The "fiery points" of her hair appear to "glow" into these words:

"You have cause to love me, I did enter you in my heart
Before ever you vouchsafed to ask for the key."

These and other lines indicate that the wife's love remains unreturned by her husband: in *The Duchess of Malfi,* as the Duchess spoke these words, her husband Antonio had disappeared, and her brother and enemy, Ferdinand, had taken a position behind her in order to stab her.

In Eliot's poem, the husband's thoughts do finally find expression in unspoken words that suggest a longing to escape a loveless marriage:

My thoughts in a tangled bunch of heads and tails
One suddenly released, fell to the floor
One that I knew:
"Time to regain the door".
It crossed the carpet and expired on the floor.

The husband contemplates the possible results if he said "I love you" or "I do not love you," and finds no essential difference:

And if I said "I love you" should we breathe
Hear music, go a-hunting, as before?
The hands relax, and the brush proceed?
Tomorrow when we open to the chambermaid
When we open the door
Could we address her or should we be afraid?
If it is terrible alone, it is sordid with one more.

If I said "I do not love you" should we breathe
The hands relax, and the brush proceed?
How terrible that it should be the same!
In the morning, when they knock upon the door
We should say: This and this is what we need
And if it rains, the closed carriage at four.
We should play a game of chess
The ivory men make company between us
We should play a game of chess
Pressing lidless eyes and waiting for a knock upon the door.

Here again, many lines survive in Part II of *The Waste Land* in what is essentially the same situation, a marriage filled with more anguish than love, with the wife making demands that the husband cannot fulfill. In "The Death of the Duchess," the husband leaves the wife to her fate. After considering the unpalatable alternatives of love, no-love, the unspoken thought that had expired revives and recurs: "Time to regain the door." The end of the poem shows that the husband has departed, and that the wife has somehow met her fate suggested in the title, "The Death of the Duchess":

Then I suppose they found her
As she turned
To interrogate the silence fixed behind her.

In the context in which we have been reading Eliot's early poetry, it would not be difficult to see this poem as in some obscure sense a fantasizing on the part of the poet about the possible solutions to his insoluble dilemma. Here he walks out the door and away from a woman who is demanding a love from him that he knows he cannot give. And in some way his departure precipitates the events that bring about her death—which he apparently desires, at least at the deepest levels of consciousness. In a way, the husband-speaker in "The Death of the Duchess" suggests strongly that his thoughts are an entangled animal mass, even unrecognizable to him, uncontrollable and operating on brute level—like monkeys hanging in clusters from the chandelier (a set of images, incidentally, for which "In the Cage" would have been an apt title). Among the tangled mass of heads and tails, thoughts of separation and even murder lurk. The irrational violence, lust, and murder of *The Duchess of Malfi* present an appropriate context for this modern tale of suburban Hampstead, but of course the differences between play and poem underscore the irony the poet cultivates.

By the time "The Death of the Duchess" was mined for lines and images in Part II of *The Waste Land,* Eliot was ready to divulge—though tortuously—more motivation for the husband's disaffection from his wife, motivation that does not seem to emerge so clearly in the earlier poem. The opening thirty-five or so lines incorporate much of "The Death of the Duchess," but in *The Waste Land* the emphasis shifts from the husband to the woman, and the supersensuous imagery suggests overpowering female sexual desire. The scene glitters as the light is reflected in marble, table, and jewels, and the "strange synthetic perfumes" hang heavily over the scene, even depressing the flames of the candle. Embedded in the setting are cupids, dolphins, and scenes from such tales as that of Philomel, brutally raped by her brother-in-law Tereus and, her tongue ripped out by her assailant, turned into a nightingale. Eliot himself in his notes calls attention to parallels with Shakespeare's *Antony and Cleopatra* and Ovid's account of Philomel in *Metamorphoses.*

Of course, we cannot take these opening lines as an objective description of the lady. It is the speaker or poet who sees, instead of her, all her rich surrounding which seems to mock him by all its sexual suggestiveness. It is he, not she, who hears Philomel turned nightingale still crying "Jug Jug, into the dirty ear of death." Eliot changed the meaning considerably when he shortened this line in the published version to " 'Jug Jug' to dirty ears." We might see that death of whatever era could be characterized as having "dirty ears"; but it is easy to assume that without death, "dirty ears" characterized the modern period, in decline from some heroic past. The "Jug Jug" in its ugliness suggests the lust that impelled Tereus to rape Philomel, that lies behind (as the speaker sees it) the temptation of the lady in this scene, that later (Part III) will be associated with the homosexual proposition from the Smyrna merchant. The extent to which the opening scene is shaped by the bias of the speaker-poet becomes manifest in the lines preceding the dialogue:

> Under the firelight, under the brush, her hair
> Spread out in little fiery points of will,
> Glowed into words, then would be savagely still.

These lines signal that we have had an exceedingly subjective description indeed, and the speaker-poet sees the lady's speeches as emanating from her strangely glowing hair.

The "conversation" (silent on the part of the poet) that follows might be construed as an intense marriage quarrel in which a distraught woman is goading her husband into speech, trying desperately to establish communication, trying to arouse him to a response, even hostile. But he remains silent, and his answers might be taken as an involuntary reaction to her staccato questions, a much more provocative and maddening reaction than overtly hostile answers would be. To the question, what is he thinking, he replies (of course silently):

> I think we met first in rats' alley,
> Where the dead men lost their bones.

By the time these lines reached publication, the first was changed to: "I think we are in rats' alley." The change may be significant. In the original, the poet appears to be reviewing his entire relationship with his wife, not just the present, and may be dropping a clue to the origin of the marriage. They "met first in rats' alley,/ Where the dead men lost their bones." Symbolically this may be taken to mean that they met during the time when the poet was plunged into gloom and despair ("rats' alley") over the death of Jean Verdenal ("Where the dead men lost their bones"). (Note, in this regard, Eliot's use of the rat imagery in "Dirge," a manuscript poem that portrays a drowned man in many of the same cadences and images as those in Ariel's song in *The Tempest*.[2]) One recent interpretation gives the imagery an explicitly sexual connotation: "The man cannot respond to her [the woman's] urgent questioning. All he can say is, 'I think we are in rats' alley/ Where the dead men lost their bones.' That is, their erections."[3] This interpretation, whatever we may think of it, appears based on an intuitive response to the poem's deeper meanings under examination here.

Immediately after this meditated "reply," the wife asks about the noise of the wind, and the husband replies that the wind is "Carrying/ Away the little light dead people." This line disappears by the time of publication, thereby diluting the poet's obsession with death as somehow involved in his relationship with his wife. The meaning of this discarded line may, as Valerie Eliot says in a footnote,[4] be related to the Paolo-Francesca episode, which takes place in the circle containing the souls of the lustful, in Dante's *Inferno* (V, 73–75); but the line might remind us, too, of the shade quoted in the Jean Verdenal dedication from Dante—the shade who forgets his "emptiness/ Treating shades as if they were solid."

After a demand from his wife as to what he knows, what he remembers, the poet affirms to himself, in lines already noted: "I remember/ The hyacinth garden. Those are pearls that were his eyes, yes!" The force of this memory is immense, and is hardly diminished by the dropping of the hyacinth garden in the published poem. It links the poet strongly with the speaker of Part I, "The Burial of the Dead," and it underscores a personal involvement (perhaps in a hyacinth garden) with Phlebas the Phoenician whose death by water is the subject of Part IV. It makes clear that the gulf separating the speaker from his wife is caused by death, and more specifically by a death with the deepest kind of personal associations, the death of someone deeply loved.

This noncommunicative conversation has wound its way to the deepest levels of the poet-speaker's suppressed feelings, and there immediately follows a kind of nervous release—"O O O O that Shakespeherian Rag—" What is left in the empty relationship between husband and wife is the meaningless activity described in the opening of "The Death of the Duchess," "hot water at ten," "closed carriage at four"—and chess. The poet muses: "The ivory men make company between us." The line was dropped, but it expressed well the vacuity of their lives together, which can be sustained only by lifeless ivory figures on a chessboard (reminders, too, of the dead men's bones that come between the two).

As companion to this upper-class social scene of husband-wife tension, "A Game of Chess" portrays a lower-class scene at a pub narrated in a monologue punctuated by a refrain from the pub-keeper: "Hurry up Please its Time." The speaker-poet does not seem to be involved in this scene, until the very end when Ophelia's line from *Hamlet* is quoted as ironic commentary on the episode: "Good night, ladies, good night, sweet ladies, good night, good night." From this close we might assume that the poet-speaker is overhearing the monologue and reporting it as he hears it, finding it an indirect commentary on his own unhappy plight. The monologuist reports a warning she gave to Lil about her husband, just returning from the service, wanting a "good time." He had given Lil some money for new teeth, but she did not have them. She had taken pills for an abortion (she already had five children), and she had never really recovered from the damage they did her. The entire passage is calculated to inspire revulsion at the sordidness of the lives of the lower orders, of those who live on an almost animalistic level, reducing all relationships to sexual, and those of the most rudimentary and elemental kind.

The passage is harsh, pitiless, ugly—and perhaps more revealing of the speaker-poet than of Lil, Albert, and their friend the monologuist. His empty relationship with his wife has colored his view of all marriage, all man-woman relationships. His imagination seizes on an overheard conversation as providing a universal insight, marriage stripped of meaning, sex stripped of joy. Although this passage is not spoken by the poet-protagonist, his bitterness and disillusion pervade it from beginning to end. In another imagination, the scene might have been shot through with genuine humor, or even with pity for the bleak plight of people living on the lower levels of society, overburdened with children, worn out with doing the dirty work of the world. But the poet's disgust lies close to the surface, and his superior view seems entirely void of feelings of compassion.

It is perhaps revealing that two of the best lines of this passage were supplied by Vivienne Eliot: "If you don't like it you can get on with it," and "What you get married for if you don't want to have children." Her sympathetic attunement to this pub scene might well suggest that she recognized something of her and Eliot's relationship even though imaginatively transferred to a radically different context, with roles reversed—the woman reluctant, the man eager. It is possible that her supplied lines remind us that Eliot had no children by his marriage, and the line about children could have come from an early confrontation of his puzzling marriage with Vivienne. But in any case, we may take the two scenes of "A Game of Chess" not so much as a commentary on modern marriage as a personal revulsion on the part of the poet-protagonist toward sexuality in marriage, a revulsion springing from his emotional paralysis caused by the death of his friend, whose memory haunts him and affects his every perception of the world. The waste land lies within.

8

In Rats' Alley

"The Fire Sermon"

to Carthage then I came, where a cauldron of unholy loves sang all about mine ears. . . .

St. Augustine

Buddha's "Fire Sermon" is a stern warning that all things are on fire, the fire of passion, the fire of hatred, the fire of infatuation, and an exhortation to "conceive an aversion" to all the senses, to become divested of passion. The "noble disciple . . . conceives an aversion for the body, conceives an aversion for things tangible." The "Fire Sermon" ends (in the translation Eliot refers to in his notes): "Now while this exposition was being delivered, the minds of the thousand priests became free from attachment and delivered from the depravities."[1]

The poet-protagonist in Part III of *The Waste Land* appears to be one who remains caught up in passion, but the examples given in the section are examples of revulsion (or hatred) rather than attraction, and particularly revulsion at the *tangibility* of women. There is strong passion throughout "The Fire Sermon," but it is the passion of a misogynist, burning with a hatred that seems almost inexplicable, except in the context we have already encountered in Parts I and II of *The Waste Land*—the protagonist held in the grip of a paralyzing memory of a dead and deeply beloved friend. It is important to note that with one exception the protagonist does not participate firsthand in the scenes of depravity portrayed in this section. Fresca appears alone (in the original manuscripts), Sweeney comes

to Mrs. Porter, the young man carbuncular couples with the bored
typist (with Tiresias as spiritual voyeur), Elizabeth and Leicester appear briefly, and the three promiscuous Thames nymphs give brief
confessional monologues without revealing the names of their sexual
partners. The one sexual scene in which the protagonist is clearly
present is the single homosexual episode in the section, the scene in
which Mr. Eugenides propositions the speaker—the final outcome of
which is not clearly related.

In the original version of "The Fire Sermon," Eliot presented a
long section of heroic couplets devoted to a lady of leisure, Fresca.
In his *Paris Review* interview, Eliot was to refer to this passage as an
imitation of Pope's "Rape of the Lock."[2] The interesting aspect of
these couplets is the way they differ radically from Pope's couplets:
Pope satirized but he also clearly sympathized with Belinda in *The
Rape of the Lock,* and the reader finds her foolish but attractive; in
contrast, Eliot savaged Fresca, rendering her in images that repel
and even revolt the reader. It is impossible to read Eliot's couplets
without feeling that they are written by a man who hates women,
and feels only revulsion at their physicality. Given the state of mind
of the poet-protagonist as we have reconstructed it thus far in *The
Waste Land,* particularly after the treatment of the women of Part II
(the "lady of situations" and Lil), we should not be surprised to come
upon such an antifeminine passage.

On awakening in the morning, Fresca "blinks, and yawns, and
gapes,/ Aroused from dreams of love and pleasant rapes." Her tea is
brought, and

> Leaving the bubbling beverage to cool,
> Fresca slips softly to the needful stool,
> Where the pathetic tale of Richardson
> Eases her labour till the deed is done.

There is an inescapably malicious note in the conception here that
betrays a deep hostility just beneath the surface-play of wit. The
function described is, after all, a natural one, and does not betray
the vulgarity the poet seems to feel, and invites us to feel. A few lines
later, Fresca eats—"Her hands caress the egg's well-rounded dome,/
She sinks in revery, till the letters come." No male reader can help

but feel uneasy at Fresca's hands on that egg's dome; the transference is an easy one, and surely intended on the poet's part: she is a female intent on seducing—perhaps emasculating—males, especially the male poet-protagonist who might be inclined to see all women, however natural in their sexuality, in some such terms. His description of Fresca emerging from the bath reinforces his misogyny:

> . . . to the steaming baths she moves,
> Her tresses fanned by little flutt'ring loves;
> Odours, confected by the artful French,
> Disguise the good old hearty female stench.

Perhaps the most revealing lines are those which take off on a series of generalizations about women:

> Fresca! in other time or place had been
> A meek and lowly weeping Magdalene;
> More sinned against than sinning, bruised and marred,
> The lazy laughing Jenny of the bard.
> (The same eternal and consuming itch
> Can make a martyr, or plain simple bitch);
> Or prudent sly domestic puss puss cat,
> Or autumn's favourite in a furnished flat,
> Or strolling slattern in a tawdry gown,
> A doorstep dunged by every dog in town.
> For varying forms, one definition's right:
> Unreal emotions, and real appetite.
> Women grown intellectual grow dull,
> And lose the mother wit of natural trull.

The choices of roles for women do not appear very great in this passage, and they all are (according to the writer) determined by that "consuming itch." We would conclude, I imagine, that since Fresca is certainly no martyr, she must be a "plain simple bitch." The syntax of the passage becomes a little blurred, but it seems that the one "definition" that is "right" for all women (or most) is: "Unreal emotions, and real appetite." The last couplet of the quoted passage seems also to rule out the possibility of women (like men, perhaps?)

becoming "intellectual," for in so doing they lose their "mother wit of natural trull," that is, natural whore. Does the passage indirectly say that women, by fact of being women, are natural prostitutes? And in turning away from this role—to become a poet, say—they lose their "mother wit" and simply grow dull? For a woman, it seems, there is no way to win!

For Fresca, it turns out, is something of an intellectual and poet. She reads the Scandinavians and the Russians, and she writes poetry:

> When restless nights distract her brain from sleep
> She may as well write poetry, as count sheep.
> And on those nights when Fresca lies alone,
> She scribbles verse of such a gloomy tone
> That cautious critics say, her style is quite her own.

Valerie Eliot reminds us in a footnote that Vivienne Eliot was something of an intellectual and poet, actually publishing a poem in *The Criterion* in 1924 containing some of the lines from this sequence of couplets on Fresca.[3] Moreover, the description of Fresca in the couplets would appear in harmony—in a rough sense—with the descriptions of Vivienne that survive from the period, such as that of Bertrand Russell (who invoked the name of a Russian writer—Dostoevsky—in an attempt to define her peculiar kind of cruelty he had observed firsthand).[4] But of course it is not necessary to identify Fresca as Vivienne to see that Eliot used some of the aspects of their relationship and his perceptions of her in the writing of his couplets about Fresca.

But Pound persuaded Eliot to remove the Fresca couplets, and they were replaced in the published poem by lines describing the river Thames as winter approaches: "The last fingers of leaf/ Clutch and sink into the wet bank." Eliot adopts a refrain—"Sweet Thames, run softly, till I end my song"—from Spenser's "Prothalamion," a marriage song focusing on beauty, purity, virginity, sung in honor of bride and bridegroom. The line can only be ironic in the context Eliot gives it. From this modern Thames, the nymphs are departed, and "their friends, the loitering heirs of city directors; / Departed, have left no addresses." The clear suggestion for the modern scene is that the "nymphs" and their friends have indulged themselves in casual sex and parted, without even knowing their partners, not to meet again. In the midst of this passage, one line flashes out with what seems clear personal reference: "By the waters of Leman I sat down and wept." Leman is the old name of Lake Geneva, used especially in Lausanne (jealous of the other Swiss city giving its name to the lake)—the place Eliot went at the time of his nervous malaise in 1921 to see a nerve specialist and to write *The Waste Land.* It appears that in this line Eliot is beginning to see himself in the role of Ferdinand Prince of Naples, weeping the loss by drowning of his father in *The Tempest* as he hears Ariel's song containing the haunting line—"Those are pearls that were his eyes." This role becomes more explicit in succeeding lines, discussed below.

Following the devastating exposure of female Fresca in the manuscripts (or the ironic "Prothalamion" in the published version), the poet-protagonist literally assumes the role of fisher-king:

> A rat crept softly through the vegetation
> Dragging its slimy belly on the bank
> While I was fishing in the dull canal
> On a winter evening round behind the gashouse,
> Musing upon the king my brother's wreck
> And on the king my father's death before him.
> White bodies naked on the low damp ground,
> And bones cast in a little low dry garret,
> Rattled by the rat's foot only, year to year.
> But at my back from time to time I hear
> The sound of horns and motors. . . .

There are so many threads of *The Waste Land* entangled in this passage that it will take a bit of discussion to disentangle them, but the task should prove worth the effort to get at obscured meaning that relates to the narrative line we have been tracking through the poem. The rat imagery echoes that in "A Game of Chess," where the poet-protagonist is goaded by his wife as to what he is thinking: "I think we met first in rats' alley,/ Where the dead men lost their bones." These lines, as well as those quoted above, suggest that the poet's dead friend and his disastrous marriage are inseparably linked, perhaps in this way: the poet's friend dies in the war, his body lying in water or mud, and the poet begins in his despair to see the world as "rats' alley"; in this state, perhaps in search of cure for his anguish, he plunges into a marriage (to a "lady of situations" or a Fresca) that exacerbates rather than heals. Some such undercurrent of meaning would account not only for the slimy-bellied rat in the passage above, but also for the lines

> White bodies naked on the low damp ground,
> And bones cast in a little low dry garret,
> Rattled by the rat's foot only, year to year.

The first of these lines evokes an image of death in war, or even Jean Verdenal's death in the Dardanelles. The bones in the garret of the second line may well be the "casting" by the poet of his anguished realization of death into a private place of the mind, where, unfortunately, it does not fade but is continuously recalled by despair (the "rat's foot" rattling the bones). The line that immediately follows these three ("But at my back from time to time I hear") evokes one of the great love-sexual poems of the English language, Andrew Marvell's "To His Coy Mistress," suggesting that the foregoing lines on death, bones, and rats recall to the poet an opportunity of the past for sensual fulfillment that time has placed outside his grasp.

But mixed in with rats, bones, and naked bodies in the passage above are some obscure allusions that must be pursued further for a moment. The poet-protagonist has become the fisher-king of Madame Sosostris' Tarot pack, but a fisher-king who fishes in a "dull canal/ On a winter evening round behind the gashouse." He is clearly fishing near that "rats' alley" where he first met his wife, and it seems reasonably clear that in such a polluted setting, no fish are to be caught. In his footnotes, Eliot not only (and "quite arbitrarily," in his words) identified the Man with Three Staves of the Tarot pack as the fisher-king (we might guess because of the phallic symbolism of the staves), but he also flagged our attention in his prefatory comment to the footnotes to the extensive use he made of Jessie L. Weston's book on the Grail legend, *From Ritual to Romance:* "The plan and a good deal of the incidental symbolism of the poem were suggested" by the book. Later (in "The Frontiers of Criticism,"

1956), when Eliot generally repudiated his footnotes to *The Waste Land,* he added: "It was just, no doubt, that I should pay my tribute to the work of Miss Jessie Weston; but I regret having sent so many enquirers off on a wild goose chase after Tarot cards and the Holy Grail."[5]

I do not wish to rehearse all of the possible applications of the Weston book to *The Waste Land,* as the poem's commentators have exploited this source to the full. But one point seems important to the interpretation advanced here having to do with cause and effect: that is the fisher-king's sexual wound as it relates to the waste land of his kingdom. Many of the commentators have blurred the relationship so that it seems that the waste land has brought about the king's disability.[6] Indeed, the assumption that the consciousness of the poem is the norm, and that the waste land depicted in the poem is a reality, reinforces this understanding of cause and effect. Thus, the despair of the poem's central sensibility is seen as caused by the waste land of modern life that seems to spread in every direction. The interpretation advanced here seeks to reverse this traditional view of the poem, and might be supported by a fresh look at Jessie Weston's book. Early in *From Ritual to Romance,* Weston makes clear that the cause flows from the king to the land, and not the other way around. After citing one of her example romances, she says:

> Now there can be no possible doubt here, the condition of the King is sympathetically reflected on the land, the loss of virility in the one brings about a suspension of the reproductive processes of Nature on the other. The same effect would naturally be the result of the death of the sovereign upon whose vitality these processes depended.
>
> To sum up the result of the analysis, I hold that we have solid grounds for the belief that the story postulates a close connection between the vitality of a certain King, and the prosperity of his kingdom; the forces of the ruler being weakened or destroyed, by wound, sickness, old age, or death, the land becomes waste, and the task of the hero is that of restoration.[7]

Weston's book had appeared in 1920, during the time when Eliot was going through a critical psychic malaise. We might assume that he happened on the book, saw parallels between himself and the fisher-king in the book, and began to assimilate elements of the work through his imagination. The most striking parallel, perhaps, would have been his impotency in his marriage; but this would have been preceded by a deep wound, in his case the loss of Jean Verdenal, which in effect caused his impotency (though, of course, psychoanalysis would no doubt trace origins of his sexual paralysis to his childhood),[8] and his impotency plunged him into an anguish and despair which caused him to see a waste land all about him, modern London converted into Dante's hell, sexual depravity everywhere he looked—as in "The Fire Sermon" itself. In this direction in our interpretation, we seem to be at the heart of Eliot's meaning when he asserted over and over again that the poem was not social criticism but a personal "grouse against life."

But before leaving the lines quoted above, we must come to terms with another allusion that, though puzzling, ultimately can be brought into harmony with the general thrust of our interpretation. As the poet-protagonist sits fishing, he is "Musing upon the king my brother's wreck/ And on the king my father's death before him." Here the poet has slipped rapidly from Weston's *From Ritual to Romance* to Shakespeare's *The Tempest,* and he flags our attention to this shift in his notes, with a specific citation to Act I, Scene 2 (the first reference to *The Tempest* in the footnotes, although it has been quoted before). Eliot's lines echo Shakespeare's. Ferdinand, Prince of Naples, has just survived a shipwreck which Ariel had manipulated, at the bidding of Prospero, and he believes his father drowned in the same shipwreck:

> Sitting on a bank,
> Weeping again the King my father's wrack,
> This music crept by me upon the waters,
> Allaying both their fury and my passion
> With its sweet air.

The music to which Ferdinand refers is Ariel's song, a line from which we have already heard twice run through the poet-protagonist's mind:

Full fadom five thy father lies;
 Of his bones are coral made;
Those are pearls that were his eyes;
 Nothing of him that doth fade
But doth suffer a sea-change
Into something rich and strange.

Eliot's lines have departed rather widely from their source, referring to his "brother's wreck" and his "father's death." In Shakespeare, there was no brother, and the father wasn't really dead; but in Eliot's life, there had been two deaths: Jean Verdenal's in 1915, in the Dardanelles, and his father's death in 1919, which would have been fresh on his mind at the writing of *The Waste Land.* As one death includes all death, so Verdenal's death could expand to suggest not only the senior Eliot's death but all death in the waste land. But the important point about the passage under examination is that, immediately after the lines of emotional revulsion depicting the female Fresca, we have a memory intruding (as in "A Game of Chess," in response to the wife's goading, and in "Burial of the Dead," in the midst of Madame Sosostris' Tarot fortune telling) in the form of a Shakespearian line weighted with associations: "Those are pearls that were his eyes," a line which Eliot himself insisted on linking with the hyacinth garden, and with Phlebas the Phoenician, and which we have speculated may be linked in association with Eliot's memory of Jean Verdenal, in life with the hyacinth garden, in death with the drowned sailor of Part IV of *The Waste Land.* [9]

As the poet-protagonist recollects Marvell's "To His Coy Mistress," he hears at his back, not Time's winged chariot, but the sound of "horns and motors" which bring Sweeney to Mrs. Porter to what appears to be a perfunctory urban adultery, accompanied by the vulgar ballad, "O the moon shone bright on Mrs. Porter/ And on her daughter/ They wash their feet in soda water." Many readers will recognize this as a vulgarized version of the ballad of "Red Wing." [10] But Eliot tells us in a footnote: "I do not know the origin of the ballad from which these lines are taken: it was reported to me from Sydney, Australia." The note is cryptic, to say the least. And it is somewhat startling to come across an elaboration of the background of the ballad in one analysis of *The Waste Land.* In *The Creative Experi-*

ment, C.M. Bowra writes that Mrs. Porter "comes, as Eliot says, from an Australian song, though he does not add that this was the song which the Australian soldiers sang when they landed on Gallipoli in 1915, and that Mrs. Porter, who seems to have kept a bawdy-house in Cairo, was a legendary figure with them."[11] *Gallipoli. 1915.* A vulgar ballad carries the fisher-king back in memory to associations with that war-time death in the Dardanelles that appears to haunt *The Waste Land.* Probably we can never know the specifics of the association with this lusty song, but the implications in our interpretation are clear enough.

The ballad of Mrs. Porter suggests the kind of spontaneous release in emotional, almost hysterical vulgarity that comes after a moment of high tension, as in "A Game of Chess" after the memory intrudes linking hyacinth garden and the drowned man, the same kind of release as in "O O O O that Shakespeherian Rag." Here it is followed by the poignant, purifying line in French from Verlaine's sonnet "Parsifal": "O, the voices of children singing in the choirloft!" This line comes at the end of the sonnet, which in the preceding lines describes in vivid detail the Arthurian knight Parsifal's mastering of his own lust, a lust that ranges widely and includes an "inclination/ Toward the flesh of a virgin boy" who tempts him with his "thin breasts" and "pretty babble."[12] Parsifal transcends these various attractions, succeeds in healing the King, and ends in adoring the Grail—as he then hears the children's voices. Eliot himself called attention in his footnotes to his source, Verlaine's sonnet, which in its entirety appears to have relevance to the memories haunting the poet-protagonist throughout *The Waste Land,* and particularly to "The Fire Sermon," and the scene of encounter with the one-eyed merchant that quickly follows.

From the purity of the children's choir of Verlaine's sonnet we are again plunged into images of unleashed passion. In the manuscripts, we encounter fragments of the song of the raped Philomel become nightingale ("So rudely forc'd" by Tereus) twice in quick succession, separated only by the account of the poet-protagonist's encounter with Mr. Eugenides, the "Smyrna merchant,/ Unshaven, with a pocket full of currants/ (C.i.f. London: documents at sight)." Eliot must have smiled as he wrote the only footnote for this passage: "The currants were quoted at a price 'carriage and insurance free to

London'; and the Bill of Lading etc. were to be handed to the buyer upon payment of the sight draft." The note clarifies nothing, of course, of any real importance in the passage, and might succeed in mystifying the reader with details that are irrelevant to the poem. No better example exists of the evasive nature of the footnotes. The outcome of this episode is more ambiguous in the original draft than in the final version. Mr. Eugenides invites the poet

> . . . in abominable [demotic] French,
> To luncheon at the Cannon Street Hotel,
> And perhaps a weekend at the Metropole.
>
> Twit twit twit
> Jug jug jug jug jug jug
> Tereu
> O Swallow swallow
> Ter
>
> London, the swarming life you kill and breed,
> Huddled between the concrete and the sky;
> Responsive to the momentary need,
> Vibrates unconscious to its formal destiny. . . .

Other lines follow which did not survive in the finished poem, such as "London, your people is bound upon the wheel!" (See discussion of the "Wheel" in Chapter 7.) The effect of the original passage is to lend emphasis to the Eugenides encounter, with the frantic singing of the nightingale in a fragmentary context, coming immediately after it, highly suggestive as to some obscure and sordid consummation, some kind of hasty and covert fulfillment of the poet's "momentary need."

Whatever the outcome of the encounter with Mr. Eugenides, the poet undergoes a metamorphosis in the next succeeding lines into a mythic figure to witness a perfunctory seduction: "I Tiresias, though blind, throbbing between two lives,/ Old man with wrinkled female breasts." Eliot forces our attention on Tiresias by the extravagance of his footnote on him: "Tiresias, although a mere spectator and not indeed a 'character,' is yet the most important personage in the poem, uniting all the rest. Just as the one-eyed merchant, seller of currants, melts into the Phoenician Sailor, and the latter is not wholly distinct from Ferdinand Prince of Naples, so all the women are one woman, and the two sexes meet in Tiresias. What Tiresias *sees,* in fact, is the substance of the poem." Eliot goes on to quote a long passage—in Latin—from Ovid, because, he says, it is "of great anthropological interest." This footnote may well be revealing in ways that Eliot had not intended. If we look at the linkages in bald biographical terms, we may identify the one-eyed merchant as a casual London encounter who through his sexual proposition melds in the poet's mind into the Phoenician Sailor, or the lost and beloved Jean Verdenal, who is closely associated with Ferdinand Prince of Naples through the haunting line reminding the poet of Verdenal's death—"Those are pearls that were his eyes"—lines the Prince hears from Ariel when he thinks his father is dead. The women, who in Eliot's footnote are revealingly un-named, are to him "one woman"—at that point in time, his wife, whose sexual desire he cannot satisfy and whose love he cannot return. The Eliot who wrote *The Waste Land,* then, must have taken the role of Tiresias, connecting both the males and the females, insolubly linked in anguishing memory to Verdenal and in un-happy marriage to Vivienne.

The long passage from Ovid quoted in Eliot's footnote is of more than "anthropological interest." It is quite revealing of the nature the poet has assumed. Here is the Rolfe Humphries translation:

> . . . Jove, they say, was happy
> And feeling pretty good (with wine) forgetting
> Anxiety and care, and killing time
> Joking with Juno. "I maintain," he told her,
> "You females get more pleasure out of loving
> Than we poor males do, ever." She denied it,
> So they decided to refer the question
> To wise Tiresias' judgment: he should know
> What love was like, from either point of view.
> Once he had come upon two serpents mating
> In the green woods, and struck them from each other,
> And thereupon, from man was turned to woman,
> And was a woman seven years, and saw

The serpents once again, and once more struck them
Apart, remarking: "If there is such magic
In giving you blows, that man is turned to woman,
It may be woman is turned to man. Worth trying."
And so he was a man again; as umpire
He took the side of Jove. And Juno
Was a bad loser, and she said that umpires
Were always blind, and made him so forever.
No god can over-rule another's action,
But the Almighty Father, out of pity,
In compensation, gave Tiresias power
To know the future, so there was some honor
Along with punishment.[13]

In Ovid this tale leads next into the tale of Narcissus, in which Tiresias plays a minor role.

What, we may ask, is the "anthropological interest" of the Tiresias story? In *The Waste Land,* he becomes a Tiresias "throbbing between two lives." As the poet-protagonist becomes Tiresias, he seems to assume the sexual potential of male and female. It is surely significant that the speaker becomes Tiresias after the homosexual episode with Mr. Eugenides and just before portrayal of the young man carbuncular and the bored typist. Like the original Tiresias in Ovid, he has had experience in both roles, male and female. He has felt passion, in the past, for the lost Jean Verdenal, and he has, in the present, acquired a wife in the form of Vivienne Eliot. But the Ovid account of Tiresias must have attracted the attention of the poet not only because the old blind man had both female and male experience, but also because when he came to judge in the argument between Jove and Juno, he took the male god's side—that females enjoyed love more than males. This, surely, has been the view of the poet-protagonist throughout *The Waste Land,* as we have witnessed his revulsion time after time at the display of "vulgar" male-female sexuality, and as we have seen him shy away repeatedly from the male sexual role.

It is perhaps of some significance that Tiresias, although presented as a bisexual witness, seems to identify with the typist as she awaits her lover in the scene that follows his introduction:

> I Tiresias, old man with wrinkled dugs,
> Perceived the scene, and foretold the rest,
> Knowing the manner of these crawling bugs,
> I too waited the expected guest.

As the young man carbuncular goes through the predictable gestures of sexual advance, we are witnesses through Tiresias more from the female than the male point of view. The boredom bordering on contempt that the typist feels in receiving the young man carbuncular is shared by Tiresias, as he confesses:

> (And I Tiresias have foresuffered all
> Enacted on this same divan or bed,
> I who have sat by Thebes beneath the wall
> And walked among the lowest of the dead.)

The young man, in departing, is presented in the original manuscripts in gross terms, later deleted:

> —Bestows one final patronising kiss,
> And gropes his way, finding the stairs unlit;
> And at the corner where the stable is,
> Delays only to urinate, and spit.

His physicality becomes somewhat overwhelming, too much for Pound, who convinced Eliot that here he had probably gone "over the mark."

The ambivalence of the poet-protagonist's participation in this scene, through the surrogate role of Tiresias, cannot probably be finally resolved. But immediately after this episode, we find the line "This music crept by me upon the waters," returning us to the lines preceding the Smyrna merchant episode, the line pointing to Ferdinand Prince of Naples and *The Tempest,* and Ariel's song, with *its* line—"Those are pearls that were his eyes"—that leads back in memory to shipwreck, the drowned sailor, and Jean Verdenal. And these memories seem to swarm back as the scene returns to modern London, "along the Strand, up Queen Victoria Street." And then the scene shifts to a view of the modern Thames ("The river sweats/ Oil and tar"), followed by a view of the Elizabethan Thames, perhaps idealized, with Elizabeth and Leicester floating in glittering splendor. Their relationship is, as the footnote reminds us, as illicit as the relationships narrated by the three compromised Thames maidens, who detail their losses, one at Richmond, another at Moorgate, and the third at Margate Sands (before going to Lausanne in late 1921, Eliot spent some time at the seaside resort of Margate with Vivienne). As these maidens expose their illicit affairs, their lovers-seducers gone, unnamed, unknown, they also expose their emotional vacuity; they display no sense of the emotional immensity of the sex they have performed so casually—but we feel a moral intensity in the undercurrents from the poet-protagonist.

After the songs of the Thames maidens, we encounter the poet-protagonist become St. Augustine: "To Carthage then I came." In his notes, Eliot cites a reference for the passage (V. St. Augustine's *Confessions*) and quotes a longer passage: "to Carthage then I came, where a cauldron of unholy loves sang all about mine ears." John Peter, in the essay that in 1952 so offended Eliot, pointed out that in fact "Augustine 'came' twice to Carthage and that on the second occasion he had travelled to it in order to escape from the misery into which he had been plunged by the death of a friend, one with whom he had enjoyed a friendship which he himself describes as 'delightful to me above all the delights of this my life.' "[14] The events to which Peter refers appear in Book IV of Augustine's *Confessions*. Augustine describes his feelings on the death of his friend: "At this grief my heart was utterly darkened; and what I beheld was death. My native country was a torment to me, and my father's house a strange unhappiness; and whatever I had shared with him, wanting him, became a distracting torture. Mine eyes sought him everywhere, but he was not granted them." And again: "I fretted then, sighed, wept, was distracted; had neither rest nor counsel. For I bore about a shattered and bleeding soul, impatient of being borne by me, yet where to repose it, I found not. Not in calm groves, not in games and music, nor in fragrant spots nor in curious banquettings, nor in the pleasures of the bed and the couch; nor (finally) in books or poesy, found it repose."[15] Augustine's wound, like that of the poet, turned all life into a waste land, and even paralyzed sexuality, destroying the "pleasures of the bed and couch."

Beginning with the line from Augustine, "The Fire Sermon" comes to an end with a vivid fervency, mixing conflicting passionate pulls and appeals:

> To Carthage then I came
> Burning burning burning burning
> O Lord Thou pluckest me out
> O Lord Thou pluckest
>
> burning

If we ascribe, as I think we must, the intensity of these lines to the poet-protagonist, we witness him still attracted by the "unholy loves" portrayed by "The Fire Sermon": he continues "burning burning" with the passion for "things tangible," but he also prays for deliverance from the fires of his personal hell. The closing lines mingle quotations from Buddhism and Christianity, a profession of sensual involvement, a prayer for deliverance, ending without conclusion. Eliot makes sure in his footnotes that we do not overlook a deliberate intermingling: "The collocation of these two representatives of eastern and western asceticism, as the culmination of this part of the poem, is not an accident."

9

Suffering a Sea-Change
"Death by Water"

Sunk though he be beneath the watery floor,
So sinks the day-star in the ocean bed. . . .
                                        John Milton

Part IV of *The Waste Land* has, in its cryptic brevity, presented many problems to the critics. The meaning has seemed obscure, but at the same time the section has a climactic air about it, and it has been made to bear much weight in the traditional reading of the poem. In view of the emphasis placed on the section, it is startling to know that Eliot at one time was willing to drop it entirely. Pound did not like the long section leading up to it, saying on the manuscript: "Bad—but cant attack until I get typescript." After he got the typescript, his canceling marks ran riot, and before he was finished, some eighty lines had been slashed. What remained was what appeared in the published version. But Eliot was far from certain about retaining any of the passage after so much had disappeared. He wrote to Pound: "Perhaps better omit Phlebas also???" Pound replied: "I do advise keeping Phlebas. In fact I more'n advise: Phlebas is an integral part of the poem; the card pack introduces him, the drowned phoen. sailor. And he is needed ABSOLOOTLY where he is. Must stay in."[1] This reply settled the matter.

Valerie Eliot pointed out in a footnote that Eliot said this section was "rather inspired" by the Ulysses canto (Dante's *Inferno,* XXVI) and its "well-told seaman's yarn."[2] The parallels she suggests from Dante, Homer, and Tennyson do not go far in explaining the role of the section in the original version of *The Waste Land*. The original version of Section IV is worth a long look. The section had a kind of balance, divided by asterisks into three unequal sections: twelve introductory lines generalizing about "the sailor"; a long central section devoted to a strange narrative of a voyage and shipwreck at sea; and a final ten-line section about Phlebas the Phoenician that survived to be published without change. As we move from "The Fire Sermon" into the original "Death by Water," we are struck by the radical difference between the two, with "Death by Water" presenting an entirely masculine world, open-air, swept by fresh ocean breezes. Most striking is the difference between the treatment of Fresca at the opening of "The Fire Sermon" and the treatment of the sailor at the opening of "Death by Water": the poet seems bent on presenting a sympathetic portrait of the sailor, in spite of the sailor's obvious attraction to "things tangible," particularly sex.

The poet's tolerance or even admiration for the sailor (as over against his contempt for Fresca) has something to do with the sailor's life at sea:

> The sailor, attentive to the chart or to the sheets,
> A concentrated will against the tempest and the tide,
> Retains, even ashore, in public bars or streets
> Something inhuman, clean and dignified.
>
> Even the drunken ruffian who descends
> Illicit backstreet stairs, to reappear,
> For the derision of his sober friends,
> Staggering, or limping with a comic gonorrhea,
>
> From his trade with wind and sea and snow, as they
> Are, he is, with "much seen and much endured",
> Foolish, impersonal, innocent or gay,
> Liking to be shaved, combed, scented, manicured.

Before Pound decided to cut all these lines, he labored at salvaging what he could. His revisions are revealing:

> The sailor
> Ashore, in public bars or streets, retains

Something inhuman, dignified.
Drunken descends
Illicit stairs, thence to reappear,
For the derision of his sober friends,
Staggering, or limping with a gonorrhea,
Yet from his trade with wind and sea,
"Much seen and much endured",
Liking to be shaved, combed, scented, manucured.

No doubt Pound's version would have been further revised, but even so we get a glimpse here of how fast and loose he played with Eliot's meaning while trying to get rid of some of the most telling grotesqueries of word or phrase. Under Pound's scalpel the sailors lose their important affirmative attributes of Eliot's first two lines (including their "concentrated will against the tempest and the tide"), and their cleanliness is dropped from line 4; their gonorrhea is no longer "comic," and therefore more sordid (line 8); they are no longer, in the third stanza, made one with the "wind and sea and snow," but as a result emerge from their hard life with nothing much more than a frivolous (and somewhat narcissistic) intent on the full treatment at the nearest barber shop.

Clearly Pound's revisions violate the tone that Eliot established in the original, an affirmative tone meant to play against the negative tone so strongly felt in "The Fire Sermon" and all its savage female portraits. For the poet-protagonist who has appeared immediately before "Death by Water" praying to be plucked out of the burning fires of passion, the sailor's life—with all its identification with wind, sea, and snow—must appear attractive indeed, in spite of the sailor's indulgences on shore. And as we place the opening lines of Part IV in the context of the death in war of Jean Verdenal, and the transfiguration of that death imaginatively in *The Waste Land* into the drowning of Phlebas the Phoenician, for which in some sense these lines are prologue—then we can comprehend the poet's sympathies underlying his portrayal of the sailor, sympathies which Pound apparently did not comprehend.

The long sea narrative standing in the middle of the original Part IV has a number of elements that might claim our attention. First, it is "Kingfisher weather," a term that cannot in the mythic context of the poem remain simply a literal description: does it somehow suggest obscurely that here is the beginning of the journey that led to the poet's wound, his transformation into the fisher-king? The journey begins on a course from "the Dry Salvages to the eastern banks"; the place name rings bells for any reader of *Four Quartets,* who will remember that the vacation home for the Eliots in America was located in Gloucester, Massachusetts, from which could be observed out in the sea a cluster of perilous rocks known as the Dry Salvages, a sight that Eliot would have remembered from his boyhood. This biographical element (to be cut out by Pound) tends to connect this section with the discarded opening lines of the first section of the original *Waste Land,* the lines presenting a group of young college men out on the town in Boston, spending the night in good-natured masculine debauchery. But the Dry Salvages signal an earlier period in Eliot's life, a time of even greater innocence and freedom.

The bizarre nature of the sea narrative that follows encourages the reader to see it as in some sense a symbolic dream, with the poet-protagonist setting out from his youthful home near the Dry Salvages. By the time we reach line 7 of the narrative, we are told that "the sea rolled, asleep." A later reference (line 60 of the narrative) to "the dream" supports the possibility of this interpretation. We might imagine that the poet-protagonist is, in his dream of a voyage·at sea, passing through the "stages of his age and youth" like the drowning Phlebas the Phoenician. Almost immediately, at the beginning of the voyage (in dream fashion), "everything went wrong": the "gaffjaws/ Jammed," and the "garboardstrake began to leak," all the food spoiled and the water turned brackish, and "Two men came down with gleet" (gleet: a "morbid discharge," and also "chronic gonorrhea"). The ship would not "sail to windward," and the crew and the sea moaned.

But just as suddenly as the troubles began, they seem to disappear, dreamlike: "Then came the fish at last." For a brief time there is harmony and fulfillment on board, as the men catch the fish in their nets and think of "home, and dollars, and the pleasant violin/ At Marm Brown's joint, and the girls and gin." After all the previous references in *The Waste Land* to the legend of the fisher-king, a scene of fish-catching must have some symbolic meaning. If we see the start of the voyage as Eliot's boyhood (when a "porpoise snored upon the phosphorescent swell"), and the first disastrous stage of the voyage as the onset of puberty and sexual turbulence and search (as in that opening discarded Harvard-Boston scene), then we might see this brief period of plentiful fish, bringing harmony to the crew, as the period of abbreviated fulfillment Eliot experienced in Paris, 1910– with his friend Jean Verdenal.

But success in the fishing is very short-lived indeed, and it is the poet-protagonist who (using "I" for the first time in the narrative) seems to signal another shift in the crew's fortunes, dreamlike in its suddenness:

> I laughed not.
> For an unfamiliar gust
> Laid me down. And freshened to a gale.

The poet seems touched by death here (the "unfamiliar gust"; cf. the wind at the door in "A Game of Chess"). In the lines immediately following, the storm at sea threatens to annihilate the entire ship with its crew. As the sea grows louder in its threats ("the horror of the illimitable scream"), the crew becomes silent in its fear, the members refusing to speak or to look at each other—another surrealistic, dreamlike scene. At this point the poet-protagonist has a strange vision:

> One night
> On watch, I thought I saw in the fore cross-trees
> Three women leaning forward, with white hair
> Streaming behind, who sang above the wind
> A song that charmed my senses, while I was
> Frightened beyond fear, horrified past horror, calm,
> (Nothing was real) for, I thought, now, when
> I like, I can wake up and end the dream.

The parallel with Ulysses' account of the lure of the sirens is clear enough, but the passage seems to have a deeper meaning for the poet in his dream—a personal meaning that links with his sudden and soon regretted marriage to Vivienne Haigh-Wood in 1915, shortly after the death of Jean Verdenal: a marriage that did indeed cause him ultimately to feel "horrified past horror," caught in a nightmare from which he struggled to awake.

The next lines portray increasing horror as the ship moves inexorably (as in a dream) toward a "white line, a long white line,/ A wall, a barrier," clearly toward its doom. The wall is some immense, dreamlike iceberg, unavoidable, carrying polar bears, offering no way out. After a shockingly bad piece of comedy ("Where's a cocktail shaker, Ben, here's plenty of cracked ice"), the sobering voice of the poet-protagonist enters with a solemn admonition: "Remember me." And in two lines set off from the narrative we have a final comment from the narrator:

> And if *Another* knows, I know I know not,
> Who only know that there is no more noise now.

If we have been interpreting the narrative appropriately (or approximately so) in its symbolic meanings, this final catastrophe in which the ship is wrecked on the iceberg brings about the symbolic death of the poet-protagonist. The first of these two lines suggests a despair beyond religious reconciliation (whatever *Another* might know; this *Another* has precedence in Dante's *Inferno*, Canto XXVI, line 129); and the second suggests an interior death, a numbness that puts him beyond the reach of the "illimitable scream" heard leading up to the lure of the sirens. He is, in short, in that state of nervous collapse ("emotional derangment") he felt that brought about his withdrawal in 1921 to Lausanne and the treatment of a psychologist and the writing of *The Waste Land*.

There remain, however, the lines about Phlebas the Phoenician. The tortuous path leading to these lines compel exploration. We have already noted the fascination death by drowning held for Eliot, as it appears repeatedly in both images and allusions in his early poetry as well as throughout *The Waste Land*. There is no need to search out every instance, but some examples are worthy of special note. There is, of course, the drowned figure washed "tip to tip" that we have commented on in the suppressed "Ode." And at the end of the *Waste Land* manuscripts are three unfinished fragments that seem to lie behind (in some obscure way) Phlebas the Phoenician. Two of these are variants of a single poem, "Dirge,"[3] which draws Pound's comment, "doubtful," indicating that it was at Pound's suggestion that it was eliminated from the published *Waste Land* volume. It is a poem that seems to linger lovingly, almost perversely, over the disintegration of a corpse beneath the waters, in lines patterned after Ariel's song in *The Tempest:*

> Full fathom five your Bleistein lies
> Under the flatfish and the squids.
> Graves' Disease in a dead jew's eyes!
> When the crabs have eat the lids.
> Lower than the wharf rats dive
> Though he suffer a sea-change
> Still expensive rich and strange

A second stanza becomes even more explicitly gory, reducing his nose to lace, his toes to bones, his eyes to "dull surprise," with predatory lobsters scratching nearby. Clearly Bleistein (who appears also in "Burbank with a Baedeker: Bleistein with a Cigar") was not prepared for death and the decay it brings. The tone of the poem is hard to assess, and it seems a strange tribute—if it indeed is—to Jean Verdenal. Unless, that is, it is an attempt at emotional exorcism, in which the poet deliberately set out to eradicate a deep grief by describing it in unpleasant terms, the result mixing unknown quantities of guilt, of blame, of cynicism along with whatever love and anguish at loss may be implicit.

The fragment that appears as the last poem[4] in the manuscript volume of *The Waste Land* is closer in spirit to lines embedded in *The Waste Land* itself, and perhaps closer to Phlebas the Phoenician. Valerie Eliot speculates (in the footnote) that it may have been written in 1921:

> Those are pearls that were his eyes. See!
> And the crab clambers through his stomach, the eel grows big
> And the torn algae drift above him,
> And the sea colander.
> Still and quiet brother are you still and quiet

These lines are obviously closely related to the refrain that recurs throughout *The Waste Land,* the line taken over from Ariel's song in *The Tempest*—"Those are pearls that were his eyes"—beginning with Madame Sosostris' first card from the Tarot pack, the card of the drowned Phoenician Sailor. In this fragment, however, we have some insight into the meaning of this line for the poet-protagonist. Emphasis is on the disintegration of the physical body, but the line that concludes the fragment reveals the depth of feeling the obsessive image has for the poet: "Still and quiet brother are you still and quiet." The poet seems to inquire whether this drowned brother has been plucked out of the burning passions that still possess the speaker. (Note, too, the poet's use of "brother" in "The Fire Sermon": "Musing on the king my brother's wreck"; and in the manuscript version of "What the Thunder Said": "DATTA. we brother, what have we given?")

But more interesting than all these fragments that lie behind the Phlebas section of *The Waste Land* is the actual source of the lines themselves. They come from the end of a poem in French that Eliot published in his second or 1920 volume of poems. In English the poem's title is "In the Restaurant," and it presents a dramatic scene set in a restaurant with the young speaker at dinner, attended upon by an old waiter who has little to do and who appears physically repulsive, scratching, chattering, slobbering: the speaker hopes that he does not slobber in the soup. The rainy weather apparently motivates the shabby old waiter to tell the story of his initiation into sex at the age of seven, when he took refuge from a rainstorm in a wooden entanglement (willows, brambles) with a girl younger than he. She was all damp, and held the cowslips he had given her. He says: "I tickled her, to make her laugh./ I experienced a moment of power and of delirium." The speaker expresses shock to himself at such behavior at such an early age. But the old waiter explains that at the critical moment, as they were fondling each other, a large dog came—and the whole enterprise was abandoned. "That," he says, "is the hurt." At the end of the waiter's story, the young speaker seems to become irrationally indignant, upbraiding the old man for his lust, his dirtiness, and, giving him coins for a bath, says: "By what right do you pay for experiences like mine?" Immediately following come the lines about Phlebas the Phoenician.[5] This strange poem may have been in some obscure way inspired by Dante's *Vita Nuova,* as the old waiter's experience appears to be a vulgarized version of Dante's experience, at the age of nine, in his encounter with Beatrice (see especially Eliot's defense of Dante's account as psychologically realistic as a "sexual experience" in his 1929 essay on Dante).[6]

Although "In the Restaurant" is the source for what appear to be key lines in a key section of *The Waste Land,* few of the commentators on *The Waste Land* have explored the meaning of the earlier poem. An exception is George Williamson, who in his *Reader's Guide to T.S. Eliot* devotes a few pages to the short poem. His theory is that Phlebas is the old waiter, cleansed finally in his drowning.[7] But this interpretation does not come to grips with the strange response of the young man to the old waiter's tale—his fierce indignation, suggesting that he feels his own experiences have somehow been sullied by the old man's sordid confession. What, then, lies in the young man's past? Not an exact replica of the old waiter's secret sex of his youth, but another sexual experience, perhaps, involving moments that the young man cherishes (just as the old waiter cherished his) but which carry similar social disapprobation? Transfigured in the young man's imagination into something pure and ideal, this experience is exposed by the old waiter's tale as partaking of the same lust that lay behind his dallying with a girl at the age of seven.

In this line of interpretation, the passage that follows on Phlebas the Phoenician suggests a purification ritual that the young man is going through in his imagination, to restore the memory sullied by the old waiter to its original state of purity and idealism. The memory involves an experience between him and Phlebas. A literal translation from the French follows:

> Phlebas, the Phoenician, suspended 15 days drowned,
> Forgot the cries of sea gulls and the surge [swell] of Cornwall,
> And the profits and the losses, and the cargo of tin:
> A current under sea carried him very far,
> He re-passed the ages of his previous life.
> Consider therefore, that was a painful fate;
> Nevertheless, he was once a handsome man, and tall.

We might guess that part of the indignation of the young man at the waiter's perverse tale comes from the fact that he is adjusting to a loss through death of the individual involved in his own experience, and the challenge he feels is somehow to preserve the memory purified of its elements of appetite—those very elements stressed in the old waiter's tale. He is, thus, striving to become a Tennyson idealizing an Arthur Hallam, or a Dante idealizing a Beatrice, finding in the experience not lust but a surge to creativity. His shock at the waiter's tale is perhaps shock at what he might in some obscure way become. And his strange mixture of fascination and revulsion, attraction and repulsion, finds its counterpart in *The Waste Land,* perhaps, in "The Fire Sermon," in the encounter between the poet-protagonist and the one-eyed merchant, Mr. Eugenides, unshaven, offering unusual invitations in his demotic French. In both episodes the speaker seems to feel the shock of some kind of self-recognition.[8]

In translating and transferring the lines from "Dans le Restaurant" to *The Waste Land,* Eliot seemed comfortable with the total excision of the old waiter and his tale of young (if perverse) love. The lines appear to serve as some kind of profound memory for the poet-protagonist, who in the original version, as we have seen, describes a devastating shipwreck and his own death just before the drowning Phlebas appears. This reinforces, perhaps, the interpretation that the lines are embedded deeply in the poet's mind, and are associated with an experience that has become transfigured in his imagination into the key experience of his life, profoundly spiritual, with a spirituality that transcends whatever physicality formed the original basis. In shifting the lines, the cleansing of the watery death gains in emphasis, as the under-sea current is described as picking Phlebas' "bones in whispers." And he is described as "Entering the whirlpool." But though there are some changes, the two passages remain remarkably similar, and they both conclude by calling attention to Phlebas' one-time physical beauty and impressiveness. In "Dans le Restaurant," he was "a handsome man, and tall." In "Death by Water," he "was once handsome and tall as you." The fact that this physical description comes at the end and lingers in the mind after the passage is read suggests that the poet has not yet become reconciled to the loss, that he has not yet been plucked out of the burning, burning, burning depicted at the end of "The Fire Sermon."

10

A Moment's Surrender
"What the Thunder Said"

Did he live his life again in every detail of desire, temptation, and
surrender during that supreme moment of complete knowledge?

Joseph Conrad

Part V is the one sustained part of *The Waste Land* that all critics
agree was produced in its entirety at Lausanne late in 1921.[1] Moreover, according to Valerie Eliot's note, Eliot was referring to "What
the Thunder Said" when he revealed that he had his own work in
mind in writing of *"The Pensées* of Pascal": "It is a commonplace
that some forms of illness are extremely favourable, not only to
religious illumination, but to artistic and literary composition. A
piece of writing meditated, apparently without progress for months
or years, may suddenly take shape and word; and in this state long
passages may be produced which require little or no retouch."[2] As
a matter of fact, we do have some earlier drafts of "What the
Thunder Said" which show that the lines did not all flow without
difficulty or revision. But it seems likely that Part V of *The Waste
Land* was the part that came most easily to Eliot, and that Pound
found most quickly revised. He wrote on the manuscript, "OK
from here on *I think.*"

In his opening footnote to this section, Eliot wrote: "In the first
part of Part V three themes are employed: the journey to Emmaus,
the approach to the Chapel Perilous (see Miss Weston's book) and
the present decay of eastern Europe." Eliot has given us in his later
comments on the footnotes sufficient reason to be suspicious of

such a note, but a simple reading of the section should suffice to reveal that the central meaning somehow escapes Eliot's three themes. There is a basic narrative pattern for which Eliot's three themes serve simply as metaphors. The traditional interpretation, following Eliot's suggestion (later, in effect, repudiated), has mistaken the metaphors for the meaning.[3] In attempting to reconstruct that central narrative or meaning, we shall be following not the Eliot of the footnotes but the later Eliot who repeatedly insisted on the personal nature of *The Waste Land,* and repudiated interpretations that stressed social criticism.

In many ways, the various subparts of "What the Thunder Said" might best be seen as an imaginative recapitulation of the preceding parts of *The Waste Land,* with, at the end, an advance beyond them and a conclusion that is not a conclusion but an obscure beginning. Lines 322–58 of the published version, through what Eliot was to call "the water-dripping song," pick up and do variations on some of the key images—stony places, rocks—of "Burial of the Dead." Lines 359–65 reintroduce the voice of a monologuist—inquiring about "the third who walks always beside you"—that may be related to the wife of the first part of "A Game of Chess." Lines 366–84 reintroduce and extend the "unreal city" and the violet hour of "The Fire Sermon." Lines 385–94 portray the arrival at the Chapel Perilous and constitute a confrontation with images of death comparable in impact and meaning to those in "Death by Water." Lines 395–422, in many ways the climax to *The Waste Land,* present the commands of the thunder and the poet's remarkable responses, which show him struggling to come to emotional terms with his irretrievable loss. And lines 423–33, concluding the poem, portray the poet still in the role of fisher-king, reconstructing his life, both real and imaginative, out of the fragments of the ruin he has struggled throughout to comprehend and salvage.

In my analysis of "What the Thunder Said," I shall follow the structure of the published version, but I want also to explore the meanings that the manuscripts might yield. I shall, therefore, proceed by sections as outlined above, but I shall use manuscript versions unless otherwise indicated.

Lines 322–58: He who was living is now dead

The opening thirty-six lines of "What the Thunder Said" may be seen as resembling that moment in an elegy when the attempts at controlling grief for the dead are reviewed briefly before the climactic moment of reconciliation (the climactic moment in "What the Thunder Said" comes later as the thunder speaks—but it is a climax without the traditional reconciliation):

> After the torchlight red on sweaty faces
> After the frosty silence in the gardens
> After the agony in stony places

The cadences here (as well as some of the later imagery) bring to mind the opening lines of the last section of Walt Whitman's "When Lilacs Last in the Dooryard Bloom'd":

> Passing the vision, passing the night,
> Passing, unloosing the hold of my comrade's hands,
> Passing the song of the hermit bird and the tallying song of my
> soul. . . .

Eliot's sequence of "after" lines build to the revelation we already know: after all the agony and grief, "He who was living is now dead." This is the fact that cannot be changed: even Madame Sosostris' Tarot pack contained no Hanged Man—no prophecy of resurrection.

Whatever the religious meaning in Eliot's opening lines (and the lines have been analyzed heretofore primarily for specific religious symbolism), it should not be allowed to obscure what appears to be a clear personal reference to the death of Jean Verdenal, surely the central meaning of the lines (the rest metaphors). Some of the imagery lying behind these opening lines is worth disentangling for glimpses of its personal content. Among the fragments at the end of the *Waste Land* manuscripts is a version of "Song. For the Opherion" (a poem that Eliot published in a magazine in 1921, and then dismantled for lines to be used in "The Wind that Sprang up at Four O'Clock").[4] It appears to be a poem of strong physical longing (as Valerie Eliot points out, the Opherion is apparently a musical instrument):

The golden foot I may not kiss or clutch
Glowed in the shadow of the bed
Perhaps it does not come to very much [canceled by Pound]
This thought this ghost this pendulum in the head
Swinging from life to death
Bleeding between two lives

      Waiting a touch a breath

The wind sprang up and broke the bells
Is it a dream or something else
When the surface of the blackened river
Is a face that sweats with tears?

I saw across an alien river
The campfire shake the spears

      Waiting that touch
After thirty years.

All of the details of this poem may be interpreted in the biographical context which we have constructed for Eliot, his devastating loss of Jean Verdenal, his precipitous marriage to Vivienne Haigh-Wood, and his life in agony torn between revulsion toward the present and memory of and desire for the past. In the closing lines, we might assume that the "alien river" (earlier, the "sullen river") is one of the rivers of Hades (Acheron, perhaps) separating the living from the dead. What the speaker sees across the river (spears shaken by campfire) suggests, in part, the forces (including Jean Verdenal) annihilated at the Dardanelles.

This spear image turns up again in a discarded version of the opening lines of "What the Thunder Said," lines which might imply more clearly their personal origin:

    After the turning of the inspired days
    After the praying and the silence and the crying
    And the inevitable ending of a thousand ways
    And frosty vigil kept in withered gardens
    After the life and death of lonely places
    After the judges and the advocates and wardens

And the torchlight red on sweaty faces
After the turning of inspired nights
And the shaking spears and flickering lights—
After the living and the dying—

After the ending of this inspiration
And the torches and the faces and the shouting
The world seemed futile—like a Sunday outing.[5]

There is much in this passage that invites personal interpretation. In transcribing, I have adopted all the indicated revisions. But it is interesting to note that in the first line, "the inspired days" was originally "a thousand days," a period of time that we might speculate as roughly equal to the period of the Eliot-Verdenal relationship (they met some time in 1910–11, possibly reencountered in 1914, and Verdenal was dead by early 1915). Some such interpretation would explain the revision to "inspired," as the days with Verdenal and preceding his death were productive ones for Eliot poetically, and it was after his death and the marriage to Vivienne that he found himself (as he complained) unable to write. This sequence of events lends significance to the next line—"After the praying and the silence and the crying"—all of these flowing from Verdenal's death.

There are lines in this discarded passage that appear opaque. The "shaking spears" image has meaning only when viewed in its original context in "Song." The "frosty vigil kept in withered gardens" may suggest the lonely life Eliot lived after Verdenal's death: the hyacinth gardens withered, and warmth of love was replaced by a "frosty vigil"—suggesting not only aloneness but the freezing of the creative impulses. "After the judges and the advocates and wardens," a particularly unyielding line, may be obscurely related to Eliot's marriage (a civil ceremony) and his succeeding hapless relationship, and all its strains and breaks, with Vivienne. "And the torchlight red on sweaty faces": this line survived to open Part V, but its meaning is not obvious: the suggestion is a procession, maybe a funeral procession, one in which perhaps the poet imaginatively indulged himself in his attempt to exorcise the memory of Jean Verdenal. The lines of this discarded version build to an anticlimax—"The world seemed futile—like a Sunday outing"—a line that is finely ironic, but contains less intensity than the closing lines of the published opening passage:

> He who was living is now dead
> We who were living are now dying
> With a little patience.

We have already seen how the rock imagery of Eliot's discarded poem, "The Death of Saint Narcissus" (a poem we attempted to relate to Jean Verdenal), was extensively used near the beginning of "Burial of the Dead." The rock imagery reappears here and is developed extensively as a kind of litany or chant. In a footnote, Valerie Eliot quotes two letters that Eliot wrote to Ford Madox Ford. In the first (14 August 1923) he says: "There are, *I* think about 30 *good* lines in *The Waste Land.* Can you find them: The rest is ephemeral." In a succeeding letter (4 October 1923), he confesses: "As for the lines I mention, you need not scratch your head over them. They are the 29 lines of the water-dripping song in the last part."[6] The comments are supported by Eliot's letter to Bertrand Russell of 15 October 1923: "It gives me very great pleasure to know that you like The Waste Land, and especially Part V which in my opinion is not only the best part, but the only part that justifies the whole, at all."[7]

The passage Eliot clearly had in mind is that beginning "Here is no water but only rock" (line 331) and running through "But there is no water" (line 358). Eliot's opinion has not been sustained by readers of *The Waste Land.* Although these lines have been heavily annotated, they have not been especially remembered or quoted. Indeed, it is difficult to see how some of them escaped Pound's emendation or excision:

> If there were water we should stop and drink
> Amongst the rock one cannot stop or think

The second line here seems especially obvious and awkward. Eliot was surely being ironic in characterizing the lines as a "water-dripping song," inasmuch as the entire point is that there is no water to drip, and there is not much sound of song in its absence. But the meaning of the passage seems clear: the poet-protagonist is destined

for a sterile life, both personally and creatively, in a world without
Jean Verdenal and at a time when belief in resurrection or immortality, however vague, is impossible. Such a world does not even
leave him alone in his aloneness:

> There is not even solitude in the mountains
> But red sullen faces sneer and snarl

It is perhaps not too far-fetched to imagine, given the nature of
Eliot's symbolic landscape here, an oblique reference to his wife
Vivienne.

The elegiac nature of this passage is emphasized in a number of
lines that appear to have an inevitable link with Whitman's *Leaves of
Grass:*

> If there were the sound of water only
> Not the cicada
> And dry grass singing
> But the sound of water over a rock
> Where the hermit-thrush sings in the pine trees
> Drip drop drip drop drop drop drop
> But there is no water
>
> > [published version]

In a 1926 review of a Whitman biography, Eliot criticized Whitman
for his ideas, but then added: "When Whitman speaks of the lilacs or
the mocking-bird, his theories and beliefs drop away like a needless
pretext."[8] Both poems indirectly referred to may well lie behind
Eliot's lines quoted above. And it would be typical that Eliot provide
a hint in the reference to the "dry grass singing." Whitman's *Leaves
of Grass* we imagine as always green, not dry, and providing a kind of
reassuring music that must be quite different from the singing of
Eliot's "dry grass." In any event, the hermit-thrush is the bird, singing in the pines and cedars, that provides the "carol of death" in
"When Lilacs Last in the Dooryard Bloom'd," bringing about the
poet's reconciliation to Lincoln's death. And the mocking-bird in
"Out of the Cradle Endlessly Rocking," discovering the loss of his
mate, sings his song of "lonesome love," and the listening boy hears

the sea's whisper'd reply, the "low and delicious word death,/ And again death, death, death, death," a word that provides the creative key for the "outsetting bard," awakening in him his "own songs." It is not difficult to hear in Eliot's "Drip drop drip drop drop drop drop" an echo of Whitman's repeated word "death." The drop of water would provide Eliot a key, too, to his "own songs," but the drop cannot be found in the stormy place of his psychic habitation after Jean Verdenal's death. There is no water; there is no release, as there is in Whitman.

Lines 358–65: who walks always beside you?

The voice in these lines is not the poet's but someone else's, perhaps the voice of the wife as in the opening half of "A Game of Chess":

> Who is the third who walks always beside you?
> When I count, there are only you and I together
> But when I look ahead up the white road
> There is always another one walking beside you
> Gliding wrapt in a brown mantle, hooded
> I do not know whether a man or woman
> —But who is that on the other side of you?

Many of the commentators, taking their cue from Eliot's reference to the theme of the "journey to Emmaus," interpret the hooded figure here as the figure of Christ as he appears after his death and resurrection, unknown to the disciples on their way to Emmaus. This interpretation seems to be supported by Eliot's footnote testimony that the Tarot card of the Hanged Man is arbitrarily associated in his mind "with the hooded figure in the passage of the disciples to Emmaus in Part V." But in another note directly associated with the above lines, Eliot says: "The following lines were stimulated by the account of one of the Antarctic expeditions (I forget which, but I think one of Shackleton's); it was related that the party of explorers, at the extremity of their strength, had the constant delusion that there was *one more member* than could actually be counted." We have, of course, learned that we cannot rely on the notes. But one important fact often forgotten is that the Hanged Man card is missing from the Tarot cards dealt by Madame Sosostris as she tells the poet's fortune, a fact important enough to elicit her comment on its absence. Moreover, Eliot's citation of a modern story as the source of his inspiration for the passage suggests that we may not go too far astray in searching for his interest in the basic situation in his own life.

It is a safe assumption that Vivenne Eliot learned early in her marriage that she was in some obscure sense competing with someone whose presence was more felt than seen. The passage above is not so shrill as the monologue in "A Game of Chess," but there is the same nervousness and puzzlement—and nagging. Most telling, perhaps, is the line, "I do not know whether a man or a woman." The silent party in this unequal exchange surely knows, for we have just witnessed his anguish over the incontrovertible fact—"He who was living is now dead." The other who is always walking by his side is the enduring memory which will not die, a memory as intrusive in a marriage as a physical presence.

Lines 366–84: the violet air, the violet light

The next series of images relates closely to those images of horror in "The Fire Sermon," but here the experiences are generalized; the "unreal city," heretofore London, now becomes Jerusalem, Athens, Alexandria, Vienna, and London. Perhaps the most striking recurrence is the color image, violet. This image was introduced in "The Fire Sermon," just before Tiresias witnessed the scene with the young man carbuncular and the bored typist. In the manuscripts it was even more explicitly symbolic than in the published version:

> At the violet hour, the hour when eyes and back and hand
> Turn upward from the desk, the human engine waits—
> Like a taxi throbbing waiting at a stand—
> To spring to pleasure through the horn or ivory gates,

> I Tiresias, though blind, throbbing between two lives,
> Old man with wrinkled female breasts, can see
> At the violet hour, the evening hour that strives
> Homeward, and brings the sailor home from sea. . . .

The "violet hour" is, we decide as we witness the typist prepare for her lover the young man carbuncular, the hour for sexual pleasure, or fleshly indulgence. The color violet suggests, perhaps, a paling of the purple passion, and perhaps even its perversion. When the color reappears in "What the Thunder Said," it is a "violet air" that seems associated with the tumbling of towers, the fall of cities, the decline of civilizations.

Following this expansive vision there comes, in the published *Waste Land,* a sequence of grotesque images that suggest perverse temptations. But at one time it was preceded by a passage that gives the entire section a more personal dimension than it now has. One much revised manuscript page reads (I have arbitrarily chosen words [italicized] in instances where the poet had not finally decided):

> So through the evening, through the violet air
> One tortured meditation *led* me on
> Concatenated words *wherefrom* the sense *had* gone—
> —When comes, to the sleeping or the wake
> The This-do-ye-for-my-sake
> [When] to the sullen sunbaked houses and the trees
> The one essential word that frees
> The inspiration that delivers and expresses
> This wrinkled road which twists and winds and guesses:
> Oh, through the violet sky, through the evening air
> A chain of reasoning whereof the thread was gone
> Gathered strange images through which *I* walked *alone*:[9]

The experience described here is a disorienting one, and though the full meaning is not clear, we may venture a guess as to the main thrust. The poet, tortured by the agony of his loss, ventures out into the "violet air" (the place for sexual fulfillment or adventure), his purpose obscured in his own mind (the sense has gone from the "concatenated words"). Though originally motivated in his restlessness by the loss of his friend, the restlessness remains as the motivation fades into obscurity. It could have been some such disorientation that led in "The Fire Sermon" to the encounter with the one-eyed merchant, Mr. Eugenides. And it leads here along a "wrinkled road that twists and winds and guesses" through the "violet sky." There was once a "chain of reasoning," but now the "thread is gone." And the poet pushes on, alone, gathering "strange images." His search for the "one essential word that frees" reminds us that he is a poet whose creativity has been impaired, and, in a section called "What the Thunder Said," he may find that releasing word when, later, the thunder actually speaks.

The strange images that the poet gathers on the "wrinkled road" are indeed grotesque, all suggesting, one way or another, nightmarish experiences or visions vaguely associated, perhaps, with illicit sexuality. (Eliot once said that he was influenced in part by a painting from the school of Hieronymus Bosch.[10]) A woman fiddles "whisper music" on the strings of her "long black hair." "And bats with baby faces in the violet light/ Whistled, and beat their wings." Although in the final version the bats (not so unusually) "crawled head downward down a blackened wall," in the earlier manuscript versions it was a man who, "*contorted* by some mental blight," yet with "abnormal powers," creeps down a wall. Voices eerily emerge from "empty cisterns and exhausted wells." In the early manuscript version—

> A man lay flat upon his back, and cried
> "It seems that I have been a long time dead:
> Do not report me to the established world"

And in the more recent manuscript—

> The infant hydrocephalous, who sat
> At a bridge end, by a dried-up water course
> And fiddled (with a knot tied in one string)

All of these are strange images indeed, and seem gathered together in the violet light to suggest the horror of sexual temptation or sexual indulgence, which the poet can no longer connect with the "chain of reasoning" (his agonizing loss) that has brought him forth on this "wrinkled road."

On the version of the older manuscript page examined above appears a passage that might relate obscurely to Phlebas the Phoenician beneath the waters:

> As a deaf mute swimming below the surface
> Knowing neither up nor down, swims down and down
> In the calm deep water where no stir nor surf is
> Swims down and down;
> And about his hair the seaweed purple and brown.
>
> So in our fixed confusion we persisted, out from town.

It is tempting to suggest, however remote the possibility, that here the poet envisions himself imaginatively diving down beneath the waters in search of his dead friend. A problem with this reading is that Valerie Eliot dates the poem, on the handwriting, at "about 1914 or even earlier."[11] But of course this dating is highly tentative and inconclusive.

Lines 385–94: the empty chapel

If the "wrinkled road" takes the poet through a kind of hell inhabited by unnatural creatures, and represents a kind of dark night of the soul (the creatures inhabitants of his own semi-deranged psyche), the next lines winding into the mountains carry him to the chapel perilous, and direct confrontation with the source of his deep perturbation—death. Jessie Weston pointed out that the knight's entry in the Chapel Perilous is "an adventure in which supernatural, and evil, forces are engaged," and represents a kind of initiation.[12] But if our reading of *The Waste Land* is generally correct, we know that the poet-protagonist's entry into the Chapel Perilous is only a psychic encounter. Symbolically, the scene may represent the poet's recognition of the destructive forces which threatened him in the immediately preceding scenes and his coming to terms with them by coming to terms with the malaise that set him in their direction—the malaise of death, and especially one particular death. For the encounter in the Chapel Perilous is a confrontation with death. The way in leads over "tumbled graves," and the Chapel itself is an abandoned place of desolation, "only the wind's home," a reminder, perhaps, that in the poet's Tarot cards there is no Hanged Man to bring resurrection. Recognition comes: "Dry bones can harm no one." Death is a natural, inevitable, part of life, and its truth—dry bones—lies in a deserted and ruined Chapel: death is final. This initiation of the poet into the nature of death represents a coming to terms with a particular death, that of Phlebas the Phoenician.

This passage represents a kind of abbreviated elegiac reconciliation. Heretofore the grief of the poet has plunged him in despair, toward that hell populated by horrible grotesques; but now, after an initiation in the Chapel Perilous that has forced a confrontation, that bestows a new awareness, he is—partially, at least—released from the paralysis and derangement of his grief:

> Only, a black cock stood on the rooftree
> Co co rico co co rico
> In a flash of lightning, then a damp gust
> Bringing rain . . .

The "black cock" becomes simply "cock" in the revision. Crowing from its "rooftree," it is perhaps a weathervane, making mechanical sounds in attracting lightning. And the lightning does flash, heralding the waters of release. But the release is surely more than aquatic: the highly evocative imagery suggests the beginning of a return to sexual potency. One critic has remarked of this passage: "There is an end to the despair and an end to the impotence. The images for this are explicitly sexual."[13] There is a turn, surely, but perhaps it is the beginning of a slow renewal rather than a sudden and complete renewal as such—especially in view of the final state of the fisher-king presented in the closing lines of the poem, shoring up fragments against his ruin.

Lines 395–422: the Thunder speaks

As the title of Part V ("What the Thunder Said") suggests, the heart of this section—and perhaps of *The Waste Land*—is to be found in the next twenty-seven lines, but the essence appears not so much in what the Thunder says as in how the poet responds. Commentators on the poem have generally passed over these lines very quickly. But we must, in our reading, linger over them and see them in the way they emerged from the earlier drafts.

Eliot directs our attention in his footnotes to the *Brihadaranyaka-Upanishad*, 5, 1, for the source of his "Datta, Dayadhvam, Damyata," and for the "fable of the meaning of the Thunder." In the *Upanishad*,[14] the god Prajapati is asked by his sons of three classes—gods, men and Asuras—to instruct them, and he does so through the voice of the Thunder, always in a single syllable. First he says "Da," and the gods understand him to advise self-control; his next "Da" to the men they take to mean "give"; and his third "Da" to the Asuras (Hindu evil deities) they understand to mean "have compassion." As the commentator on this *Upanishad* points out, the uttering of the one syllable forced each group in turn to discover his own weakness within. In other words, the god's advice turns out to be self-advice that is elicited through self-awareness.

Eliot departs from the *Upanishad,* as he inverts the order from *control yourselves, give,* and *have compassion* to *give, sympathize, control,* and as he subtly modulates the meaning to suit his own purposes. The first "Da" the poet hears he takes to be "Datta": give. Whereas the men in the *Upanishad* take this advice to mean "distribute your wealth to the best of your might, for you are naturally avaricious," Eliot applies it in an entirely different context. This should be sufficient signal to the reader that the poet is not simply reproducing the incident from the *Upanishad,* but is adapting it to his situation in *The Waste Land.* When the Thunder says "Da," the poet-protagonist responds with a genuine confrontation with the interior self—and the intrusive memory that has haunted him throughout the poem.

The manuscript is helpful in clarifying the nature of that memory. At one time (in probably the earliest version), Eliot had written (italicized words later revised):

DATTA. *we brother,* what have we given?
My friend, *my friend, beating in* my heart,
The awful daring of a moment's surrender
Which an age of prudence *cannot* retract—
By this, and this only, we have existed,
Which is not to be found in our obituaries,
Nor in memories *which will busy* beneficent spiders
Nor *in documents eaten* by the lean solicitor
In our empty rooms.

Nothing of a "hyacinth girl" here! As G. Wilson Knight emphasized in his 1972 *Denver Quarterly* essay, the partner is unmistakably masculine.[15] The moment is a "moment of surrender," a giving of the self to a friend—a surrender and a giving that "an age of prudence cannot retract." In revising the passage, the meaning was not changed, but slightly dispersed or diffused. The first line dropped the direct address, "we brother," the second line became "My friend, blood shaking my heart"; in the original, it is clearly the friend "beating in" the poet's heart that has been related to his "emotional derangement," and which he is willing to confront directly here for the first time.

A glance at what earlier commentators did with this passage reveals the difficulties posed by the traditional interpretations. Cleanth Brooks (1939) wrote; "Here the larger meaning is stated in terms which imply the sexual meaning. Man cannot be absolutely self-regarding. Even the propagation of the race—even mere 'existence'—calls for such a surrender. Living calls for . . . belief in something more than 'life.' " George Williamson (1953): "Their giving has been a surrender to passion, not love—as the poem abundantly illustrates. Yet, while self-regarding, this is their only evidence of life or existence." Grover Smith (1956): "The first [command] surely concerns the sexual blunder to which Tiresias has already confessed. The surrender has involved no acceptance of love, of the demands of life, but a yielding to lust." Hugh Kenner (1959): "The first surrender was our parents' sexual consent; and when we are born again it is by a new surrender, inconceivable to the essentially satiric sensibility."[16] The astonishing thing in all this commentary is the number of words devoted to explanations that obscure rather than clarify meaning. There is basic misunderstanding that the relationship portrayed is between the poet-protagonist and his friend, the commentators insistent on glossing over the clear male-male—not male-female—relationship.

The meaning of the passage appears to me lucid, and the tone not ironic but deeply moved, deeply moving. It is a confrontation that is also a confession. The poet and his friend have experienced the "awful daring of a moment's surrender." An age, or lifetime, of "prudence" cannot "retract" that moment, cannot replace it: it exists, it endures in the memory. Moreover, this moment has been the essence of their existence, this memory shaping their very selves, giving them their essential, their emotional identity. When they die, this shaping event will not even be listed in their obituaries, nor will it be found in "memories" (mementoes, "treasures") that the spiders will take over, nor in the documents, "under seal," opened after their death by their lawyers (solicitors) going through their "empty rooms." Clearly this passage is clarification for the self, and an affirmation, a confrontation with the truth that the poet-protagonist must learn to live with, not evade, not suppress, not deny, not duplicate or attempt to duplicate with some unsavory one-eyed merchant.

The second "Da" of the Thunder becomes in the poet's understanding "Dayadhvam," "sympathize." The manuscript version is again helpful (italicized words later revised):

> Dayadhvam. *friend, my friend* I have heard the key
> Turn in the door, once and once only.
> We think of the key, each in his prison,
> Thinking of the key, each *has built* a prison.
> Only at nightfall, aetherial murmurs
> *Repair* for a moment a broken Coriolanus. . . .

Once again, Eliot's revisions have slightly diffused the meaning. And his quotations in the footnotes from Dante and F.H. Bradley have deflected the critics from the continuity of meaning in the Thunder passage. It is significant, as revealed in the manuscript, that the passage begins in direct address to the friend. The key that has turned in the door "once and once only" is surely related to the previous "awful daring of a moment's surrender." The self has been genuinely penetrated only once—during that surrender with the friend. The rest of existence has been a memory of that moment, and a contemplation of the key that was once turned. But each is in his prison, a prison (as in the manuscript) "each has built." Though we long for that human or spiritual intermingling, for the soul-sharing that might come with the turn of the key, it does not turn, and we remain alone. *Sympathize. Have compassion.* In a world in which we all exist behind barriers, in fearful isolation, that we ourselves have created, where the very nature of existence itself helps create the prisons for ourselves we build, there is abundant need of sympathy and compassion.

The manuscripts reveal that the image of Coriolanus was one of the most troublesome for Eliot, as well it might have been. From "repair" he changed to "Restore," and then to "Revive the spirits of. . . . " Finally the line read: "Revive for a moment a broken Coriolanus." If we have read Eliot's suppressed "Ode" properly, we have seen the Coriolanus there functioning in allusion, however tortuously, to the death of Jean Verdenal—or the death of those in battle. From these passages it appears that Coriolanus (like the unlikely Phlebas the Phoenician) was associated for Eliot in some obscure way with Jean Verdenal, like Coriolanus a victim of his country's wars. Whether a commander at the Dardanelles (and some of the Allied generals were endowed with the arrogance of a Coriolanus) or Verdenal himself, this modern Coriolanus can be revived only at nightfall, in "aethereal murmurs." The single moment, that one turn of the key, returns only imaginatively, in association with images indelibly if obscurely connected with the memory of that singular time.

The third "Da" spoken by the Thunder evokes from the poet "Damyata," control. In the *Upanishad,* the control is clearly self-control. In Eliot, the control is expanded in meaning. Again, the original manuscript gives us more details with which to reconstruct the meaning (italicized words later revised):

> Damyata. *the wind was fair,* and the boat responded
> Gaily, to the hand expert with sail and *wheel.*
> The sea was calm, *and* your *heart responded*
> Gaily, when invited, beating *responsive*

> To controlling hands. *I left without you*
> *Clasping empty hands, I sit upon the shore*
> *Fishing, with the desolate sunset behind me*
> *Which now at last. . . .*

These lines went through several changes, and were finally published:

> *Damyata:* The boat responded
> Gaily, to the hand expert with sail and oar
> The sea was calm, your heart would have responded
> Gaily, when invited, beating obediently
> To controlling hands

In the published *Waste Land,* there is a distinct break at this point, as the image of the poet become fisher-king begins the concluding section of the poem.

Given the sequence we have been following in the manuscripts, there is every reason to believe that the poet is addressing his friend in this sea-scene, and it may, in the original version, have been a reconstruction of that moment of daring surrender. In the original manuscript, the moment is consummated: " . . . your heart responded/ Gaily, when invited, beating responsive/ To controlling hands." By the time the passage is published, the moment is an opportunity passed by: " . . . your heart *would have* responded"; and the beating of the heart would not have been *responsive* but *obedient.* The "controlling hands" are curiously retained. Moreover, the original manuscript describes a separation: "I left without you/ Clasping empty hands, I sit upon the shore." That "desolate sunset" is clearly the poet's own desolation in the separation from his friend, symbolized by the "Clasping empty hands" that once were "controlling."

The third "Da" completes the Thunder's message, and completes, too, the poet's vivid confrontation with the realities of his life that he had heretofore evaded. Though he has not escaped his agony, he has come to a full recognition of its causes, and he can now set about shaping his life to live as he can with it. We might summarize the section devoted to the "fable of the meaning of the Thunder"—give, sympathize, control—thus: the poet-protagonist confesses that he has given himself in surrender in a moment whose meaning is beyond calculation; he asks for understanding and sympathy in his impenetrable isolation, an imprisonment that is part of the common human predicament; and he pledges an exchange of one kind of control (of another) into self-control, changing controlling hands into clasped hands.

Lines 423–33: these fragments I have shored against my ruins

The manuscripts show that the fisher-king of the last lines was clearly the occupant of that boat in the preceding lines, and that it is he who has felt sharply the separation from the friend depicted in the Thunder fable. In going about to set his "lands in order," he is in effect putting his life together again. Almost immediately, however, a nonsense refrain intrudes, linking this moment of emotional intensity to the moment when "O O O O that Shakespeherian Rag" or "O the moon shone bright on Mrs. Porter" invaded the consciousness of the poet: "London Bridge is falling down falling down falling down." We realize, of course, that more than London Bridge is falling down for the poet. his whole life is collapsing (as it seemed to be when he went to Lausanne in 1921), and he is searching for the means of propping it up again. As we read on to discover the materials to be used, we enter some of the most highly allusive and provocatively obscure lines in English poetry. Since the quoted passages are the fragments with which the poet proposes to shore "against his ruins," we would do well to look at them rather closely. The commentators have gone through them, of course, but have (as usual) found what they were looking for to prop up their own interpretations.

    The first line quoted is "Poi s'ascose nel foco che gli affina": "Then he plunged back into the fire that refines [purifies] them." This line refers to the twelfth-century Provençal poet Arnaut Daniel, who appears at the end of Canto XXVI of Dante's *Purgatorio*. This canto is, significantly, the canto of "The Rein of Lust," and in it there is a vivid account of Arnaut Daniel's band of the hermaphroditic lustful (line 82: "Nostro peccato fu ermafrodito"; "Our sin was hermaphrodite") encountering and kissing a band of sodomites and then passing on in the refining fire. There are other such sensational details in this interesting canto. For some reason, this canto was one of Eliot's favorites, and he used it again and again in his poetry (see discussions in Chapters 4, 5, and 11; see also Chapter 4, note 10). In quoting the last lines of it, referring to Arnaut Daniel, he seems to be suggesting that the poet-protagonist of *The Waste Land* is also passing through the refining fire in penance for his lust—as in "The Fire Sermon" and also in the landscape of horror, with its "violet air," in "What the Thunder Said."

The second quotation, part Latin and part English, comes from an anonymous Latin poet of the first or second century of the modern era, entitled *Pervigilium Veneris,* or *The Vigil of Venus,* a long poem celebrating the experience of love and sex. The line "When shall I be like the swallow—O swallow swallow" is Eliot's abbreviation and slight change of the original line: "When shall I be like the swallow and my voice no longer dumb?"[17] The poet of *The Vigil of Venus* is wondering when he will be violated like Philomela and motivated to song (the story of Tereus and Philomela is briefly retold in the preceding stanza); as, perhaps, the poet of *The Waste Land* is wondering when he will regain his poetic gift, stilled with the death of his friend and the advent of his unhappy marriage. Each verse of *The Vigil of Venus* ends with a refrain, and the last stanza containing the quotation Eliot used ends: "Hast thou known love's joy and sorrow? Love be thine again tomorrow!" This seems to be the prayer of the poet, a prayer for return of the ability to love.

The third fragment comes from a sonnet by the early nineteenth-century poet Gérard de Nerval, "El Desdichado,"[18] the Spanish title meaning "The Unfortunate One" or "The Outcast." The speaker of this poem is clearly identifiable as Nerval, and the poem is filled with personal references, primarily to agonies suffered because of unfulfillment in love. The opening lines read:

I am the dark man, the disconsolate widower,
The prince of Aquitania whose tower has been torn down:
My sole *star* is dead,—and my constelled lute
Bears the black *sun* of *Melancholia.*

Nerval never married, but the loss of his love he could feel so severely as to feel himself a "widower." The "*star*" that is dead is usually identified as the actress Jenny Colon, whom he loved and then lost, idealizing her later in his poetry—which, as a result, is a poetry (like "El Desdichado") of melancholy. Nerval really fancied himself a descendant of an aristocratic family whose "towers" in Aquitania had disappeared long before; thus he is disinherited, cut off from his roots and traditions. It is easy enough to see the basis of the *Waste Land* protagonist's identification with the persona of "El Desdichado." Given the obscurely sexual preoccupations of the speaker of both poems, the line referring to the destruction of the tower of the prince of Aquitania seems to take on a fairly clear sexual suggestion—that is, sexual disability, phallic failure, a tower that is down. The miserable speaker of the Nerval poem lives with his memories:

> Crimson the queen's kiss blazes still upon my face.
> The siren's naked cave has been my dreaming place.

But now, the speaker lives in the "midnight" of his grave. The application to the *Waste Land*'s poet-protagonist become impotent fisher-king would appear clear.

"These fragments I have spelt into my ruins": this first version of a famous line places emphasis on the speaker as poet, a poet searching for phrases and lines to place in (spell into) the poem—*The Waste Land*—that represents his ruins, his personal disintegration. Some of the personal suggestion of the line faded, perhaps, when it was turned into the now familiar: "These fragments I have shored against my ruins." These fragments, from three different languages, three different historical periods, recapitulate the poet-protagonist's personal situation, his longing for the refining fire of purification, his longing for the return of his creative gift through a new love, his longing for the return of his virility and potency. There is little of religion or civilization, much of love and sex in the fragments, contrary to their traditional reconstruction in the commentaries. In short, tracked to their contexts, these fragments support Eliot's position that his poem is not a piece of social criticism but in some sense a personal drama.

The next quotation that appears—"Why then Ile fit you. Hieronymo's mad againe"—consists of two fragments from Thomas Kyd's sixteenth-century play *The Spanish Tragedy*. Hieronymo is driven near madness in his grief at the murder of his son, and he plots the revenge killing of the murderers. His opportunity arrives when the murderers ask him to supply a play for the court, and he agrees, seeing an opportunity to destroy them while "fitting" them—accommodating to their plans:

> Why then I'll fit you; say no more.
> When I was young I gave my mind
> And plied myself to fruitless poetry. . . . (P. 105)[19]

The context here suggests that the poet-protagonist of *The Waste Land* sees himself indirectly in the role of Hieronymo, driven like him in deep grief to a near madness over the loss through senseless death of someone beloved beyond reason. In *The Spanish Tragedy*, Hieronymo fashions his play to shadow forth, obliquely and enigmatically, the actual situation in which his son has lost his life—as Eliot's *Waste Land* indirectly dramatizes his own personal experience in veiled scenes and indirect images. Moreover, Hieronymo insists that his drama will be played in "unknown languages," including Latin, Greek, Italian, and French. His actors (and victims) are understandably puzzled by this insistence, but he reassures them that at the end he will appear and "make the matter known./ And all shall be concluded in one scene" (p. 110).

The play is played out, and the murderers of Hieronymo's son are, in accordance with the plot, killed on stage, one by Hieronymo himself. At the end Hieronymo stands forth to explain that the killings have not been feigned but real, and then, describing himself as "The hopeless father of a hapless son," he has his dead son brought on stage to reveal all the meaning of the play and the plot it concealed (p. 117). In *The Waste Land*, which is composed in part (as every reader knows) in "unknown languages," the poet-protagonist appears by them and other means to conceal more than he reveals—until the end, when in response to the Thunder's voice, he makes a kind of direct revelation of "the awful daring of a moment's surrender." As Hieronymo in *The Spanish Tragedy* is pursued off stage and commanded to confess, he bites off his tongue, and this act reminds us of the *Waste Land* poet's concern for his creativity, manifest in the fragment remembered from *The Vigil of Venus*—"When shall I be like the swallow and my voice no longer dumb?" Perhaps in coming to psychic terms through the writing of *The Waste Land* with the experiences he has heretofore evaded, he will rediscover his creativity, both physical and poetic.

The Thunder's voice repeats at this moment—Datta. Dayadhvam. Damyata: Give, Sympathize, Control. These commands have brought about the direct confrontation with the truth of the poet's past, and the commands and his responses must remain in his consciousness as the way to the cure for his impotence as fisher-king and as the means for restoring his voice as a poet. Only by such confrontation and salvaging of the self can the poet-protagonist come to fruitful terms with his malaise, his "emotional derangement," and find his way to the peace he seeks. As he continues to shore his fragments against his ruins, he may restore the self he has lost, and find the peace he seeks: "Shantih shantih shantih"; "The Peace which passeth understanding," as the poet so conveniently tells us in his final footnote. And we can almost hear the sigh of longing that must have hovered over it as he wrote.

11

Funerals and Farewells
"Exequy" and "Elegy"

Be mindful in due time of my pain.
In thought I see my past madness.
Dante's Arnaut Daniel

As we have seen in examining the manuscripts of *The Waste Land*, there are several poems and poem fragments published with the long poem, some of which were mined for passages, but others of which were left unused and unpublished. In Pound's letter of 24 December 1921, to Eliot on *The Waste Land*, he referred to the "superfluities":

> I think your instinct had led you to put the remaining superfluities at the end. I think you had better leave 'em, abolish 'em altogether or for the present.
>
> If you MUST keep 'em, put 'em at the beginning before the "April cruelest month." The POEM ends with the "Shantih, shantih, shantih."
>
> One test is whether anything would be lacking if the last three were omitted. I don't think it would.[1]

Eliot's reply made clear that he was quite willing to let the extra poems go: "Certainly omit miscellaneous pieces."[2]

There is some uncertainty as to just which three poems Pound was referring to. We might eliminate first a number of fragments that appear without title, some of them clearly early drafts of portions of

The Waste Land. These fragments are listed by their first lines in the table of contents: "After the turning of the inspired days" (used in part for Part V); "I am the Resurrection and the Life"; "So through the evening, through the violet air" (used also in Part V); "Those are pearls that were his eyes. See!" (used as a recurrent image through-out).

There are six poems with titles among these fragments, and two of these can be eliminated because several of their lines were used in the finished *Waste Land*. "The Death of St. Narcissus" supplied a number of lines ("Come under the shadow of this grey rock") to Part I. "The Death of the Duchess" yielded many of its lines ("Under the brush her hair/ Spread out in little fiery points of will") to the first half of Part II. There remain four poems for our speculation: "Song," "Exequy," "Elegy," and "Dirge." Pound's letter makes clear that two of the three poems Eliot had proposed to publish with *The Waste Land* were "Song" and "Exequy": "The song has only two lines which you can use in the body of the poem. The other two, at least the first, does not advance on earlier stuff. And even the sovegna [used in "Exequy"] doesn't hold with rest; which does hold."[3]

In her footnote to "Dirge," Valerie Eliot says: "This is probably the third of the miscellaneous poems rejected by Pound (the other two being *Song* and *Exequy*."[4] She does not give her reasons for her speculation. But on the manuscript of "Dirge" there is the notation, "doubtful," which appears to be in Pound's handwriting. However, Pound also made revisions of "The Death of the Duchess," even though it was not apparently under consideration for inclusion. In "The Making of *The Waste Land*," Grover Smith concludes that the third poem was not "Dirge," and, "at the risk of perversity," nomi-nated another candidate: "This is 'Elegy,' an otherwise unplaced draft whose presence in the manuscript is unexplained except that it is tied to 'Dirge': these two were written on opposite sides of the same sheet."[5]

My own judgment is that "Dirge"[6] (which opens "Full fathom five your Bleistein lies," clearly a satiric use of the Ariel song from *The Tempest*) would have been slightly out of harmony with *The Waste Land,* somewhat diminishing the serious use throughout the main poem of that haunting line "Those are pearls that were his eyes," taken from that same *Tempest* song. Eliot might well have proposed it as one of the three extra poems to be published, but I would agree with Pound's judgment of "doubtful." It appears to me to lie obscurely behind the evolution of Part IV ("Death by Water") of *The Waste Land,* and I have discussed it briefly there. In similar fashion, I see "Song. For the Opherion" (already published in 1921) as somehow lying behind the evolution (via the fragment "After the turning of the inspired days") of Part V, and I have included reference to it in my discussion of "What the Thunder Said." There remain, then, "Exequy" and "Elegy" for brief examination, especially in the ways they might relate to the poet-protagonist's voice we have been tracing in *The Waste Land.*

"Exequy" and "Elegy" make a strange pair of poems, the first imagining the speaker's own death, the second imagining the death of a "beloved"—perhaps a wife. An *exequy* is a funeral rite or obsequy, and the poem consists of an imaginative prediction of how the speaker's tomb will become a center for the worship of lovers. "Exequy"[7] opens:

> Persistent lovers will repair
> (In time) to my suburban tomb,
> A pilgrimage, when I become
> A local deity of love,
>   And pious vows and votive prayer
> Shall hover in my sacred grove
>   Sustained on that Italian air.

The poem never reveals just what in the speaker's life might cause his tomb to become the destination for lovers' pilgrimages. The tradition that the poem evokes is best represented, perhaps, by John Donne's "The Canonization," a poem in which the lover begins by protesting vehemently his love ("For God's sake, hold your tongue, and let me love"). But in the Donne poem, the lovers' love will be entombed in poetry:

> We can die by it, if not live by love,
>   And if unfit for tombs and hearse
> Our legend be, it will be fit for verse. . . .

In contrast with the Donne poem, "Exequy" does not portray a pair of lovers but instead presents a speaker who asserts, in a rather languid tone, that lovers will turn him into a "deity of love." He somewhat narcissistically imagines his "athletic marble form," which will present him to the lovers "Forever lithe, forever young," while the lovers hang on his tomb "grateful garlands" and "flowers of deflowered maids." He will be "A bloodless shade among the shades/ Doing no good, but not much harm." And in imagining the festivities that will take place around his tomb, he envisions their conclusion in some "invariable surprise/ Of fireworks, or an Austrian waltz." The ironic tone throughout the first three stanzas suggests a "love" poet like the author of Eliot's "Ode":

> Misunderstood
> The accents of the now retired
> Profession of the calamus.

The poem up to this point does not seem to have much impact, but the fourth stanza presents an interesting turn that places it in the context of our *Waste Land* discussion:

> But if, more violent, more profound,
> One soul, disdainful or disdained,
> Shall come, his shadowed beauty stained
> The colour of the withered year,
>   Self-immolating on the Mound
> Just at the crisis, he shall hear
>   A breathless chuckle underground.
> SOVEGNA VOS AL TEMPS DE MON DOLOR.
> Consiros vei la pasada folor.

Valerie Eliot's note translates the final couplet: "Be mindful in due time of my pain./ In thought I see my past madness."[8] The lines come from the by now familiar Canto XXVI of Dante's *Purgatorio*, the canto of "The Lustful." The lines are quoted out of order, the first being line 147, the second line 143, and they come from Arnaut Daniel's speech at the end—that same passage that gave *The Waste Land*'s fisher-king one of the fragments to "shore against his ruins"— "Then he plunged back into the fire that refines them."

If we place "Exequy" in the context of *The Waste Land* (where Eliot first thought of placing it), we quickly identify the speaker of the poem with the poet-protagonist of *The Waste Land*. The basic irony of the poem becomes immediately clear: this "deity of love" is one who could not love women, one who would no doubt express boredom with the "flowers of deflowered maids" brought to his tomb. His feelings can become engaged only when his tomb is visited by "one soul" who is "more violent, more profound," who clearly is unhappy because he has been either "disdainful or disdained," passing love by, and who has now, perhaps, grown old—his beauty "stained/ The colour of the withered year." The response of the poet-protagonist is to give forth a "breathless chuckle." The joke is on the "self-immolating" individual who has come to the "deity of love" for relief of a misery which in fact is matched by the deity's own pain. "Be mindful in due time of my pain," he says. "In thought I see my past madness." The madness, perhaps, of "The awful daring of a moment's surrender"? Or the madness of separation, departure, "Clasping empty hands"? The pain may be twofold: the pain of the memory of "surrender," but also the pain of the memory of renunciation. It is, of course, tempting to identify the "disdainful or disdained" individual as someone important in the poet-protagonist's own emotional life—even the one who, after that single "moment's surrender," became disdained, renounced. But the poem does not offer enough evidence for any firm conclusion.

"Elegy"[9] envisions not the poet's death but the death of someone close, the precise identity blurred by the imagery of dream. There may be a number of ways of reading "Elegy," but at least one way is to see the speaker of the poem as our poet-protagonist of *The Waste Land,* here grieving for his "imagined" dead wife in what might be called an "anti-elegy." The speaker breathes an "amen" in his prayers for the "parting shade," but it is a "hypocrite's amen!" The wife in a sense replays the role of Aspatia in Beaumont and Fletcher's *The Maid's Tragedy.* Abandoned by her lover for another woman, Aspatia dresses up as a man and confronts her lover as her own brother seeking revenge, and deliberately provokes her own killing. Translated into the speaker's situation, the "other woman" is the memory of the dead friend, and the killing of Aspatia may be seen simply as the symbolic or psychic killing of his wife.

In the second stanza, the speaker realizes that he "should have mourned" steadfastly at the "sinking of so dear a head"—"Were't not for dreams: a dream restores/ The always inconvenient dead." The steadfast mourning, then, is given over to an awesome direct confrontation in dream:

> The sweat transpiréd from my pores!
> I saw sepulchral gates, flung wide,
> Reveal (as in a tale by Poe)
> The features of the injured bride!
>
> That hand, prophetical and slow
> (Once warm, once lovely, often kissed)
> Tore the disordered cerements,
> Around that head the scorpions hissed!

The "injured bride" here might relate to the bride turned into a "succuba" by the bridegroom in "Ode." It apparently is the dead bride's "lovely" hand that, in the dream, attempts to tear off the "disordered cerements," and return to life—like Madeline in Poe's "The Fall of the House of Usher," who does work her way out of her burial vault and seek out her brother, Roderick Usher (who had placed her prematurely in the tomb), to carry him with her in a final climactic fall.

This dream might be indirectly revealing that the poet-protagonist's wife has, too, been buried before her death, thus intensifying the speaker's sense of guilt. And guilt he feels in abundance, for what he has done, and in not wanting it undone:

> Remorse unbounded, grief intense
> Had striven to expiate the fault—
> But poison not my present bliss!
> And keep within thy charnal vault!

It is almost as though the poet's dream is like that frightening Dog of the closing lines of Part I of *The Waste Land,* the Dog who is "friend [or foe] to men" but who might dig up that corpse that Stetson planted in his garden last year. However implicated in his wife's imagined death, he does not want her state changed to life.

The poet's "present bliss" must appear to be ironic in the fiery light of the last stanza. God pursues the poet-protagonist in a "rolling ball of fire" (a Blake-like image)—that is, pursues his "errant feet": a possible reference to feet that have strayed from the normal course of love (as perhaps in the "awful daring of a moment's surrender"). Eliot clearly had trouble making up his mind as to the nature of God's flames, settling finally on flames of "anger and desire"—but trying out "pity," "Passion," "Horror," "ire." Whatever their nature, the flames of God's "ball of fire" "approach" the poet with "consuming heat." Thus in imagining his wife's death, the poet-protagonist is left alone with the "bliss" of the memory of his dead friend, a bliss which in reality is the "refining fire" that Arnaut Daniel leaps back into at the end of his speech concluding the canto of "the Lustful," Canto XXVI of the *Purgatorio*.

There is, of course, a possible alternate reading of "Elegy," requiring only a few more flights of biographical fancy. If we assume that the parting shade is Jean Verdenal, the poet's "amen" is hypocritical because his real feeling is one of agony. The "wrong'd Aspatia" may be a more likely role for Jean Verdenal—wronged in the sense of abandoned in some obscure way by the poet, her assumption of a man's (her brother's) identity perhaps suggestive also. The second stanza, concerned with the "sinking of so dear a head," may be suggestive of the loss of Jean Verdenal as one of the "inconvenient dead." But the dreams that appear to be counted on for restoration of the dead reveal not Jean Verdenal but the "injured bride"—Vivienne Eliot, attempting to escape from the tomb, or the living death to which the poet has assigned her. Thus the dreams play a trick on the poet by haunting him with his unwanted wife.

In the next to last stanza, the poet refers to "the fault" that precipitated the unbounded "remorse" and acute "grief"—the fault, perhaps, of marrying Vivienne in a bitter aftermath of the death of Jean Verdenal. Or perhaps the "fault" goes back to a rejection at some critical juncture of Jean Verdenal, a rejection remembered in a mixture of guilt and grief after his death. In this reading, then, the poet's request that the occupant of the "charnal vault" remain there and not "poison" his "present bliss" (once "nightly bliss," more clearly sexual) must be taken as ironic. But, of course, the last stanza presenting the poet as pursued by God's "rolling ball of fire," containing flames of "anger and desire," forces an ironic reading of "present bliss." Clearly the speaker is speaking out much as Arnaut Daniel from the purifying flames of purgatory (as in Canto XXVI of the *Purgatorio*).

Our reading of "Exequy" and "Elegy" stresses their compatibility with the main thrust in the meaning of *The Waste Land.* In suggesting that Eliot drop them, Pound did not see them in conflict but rather as "superfluities"—and that perhaps they are. It must be remembered, too, that neither "Exequy" nor "Elegy" is finished, and each might well have been revised in significant ways before being published. Eliot never went back to them, or attempted to resurrect them, apparently; and it was his custom to recover previously abandoned work whenever he could. Did he think them inferior? Or did he quickly pass by their emotional significance, on to other feelings, other concerns? Or did they seem, later, to reveal too much of what he had grown accustomed to keeping buried? Whatever the case, they have their interest for anyone exploring the undercurrents of meaning in *The Waste Land,* associated as they are with it in its formative stages.

12

A Kind of Valediction
A Familiar Compound Ghost

Footfalls echo in the memory
Down the passage which we did not take
Towards the door we never opened
Burnt Norton

Although Eliot's poetry after *The Waste Land* cannot be dealt with in detail in this study, there is one passage in *Four Quartets* that appears to be a kind of coda to the Eliot-Verdenal relationship: the post-air raid scene in Part II of "Little Gidding" (1942), dramatizing an encounter with a "familiar compound ghost." Eliot criticism has suggested various candidates as the original for this enigmatic figure, but there has been general recognition that a ghost that is "compound" was probably an assimilation of several identities. One of these, and perhaps the primary one, I believe, appears to be Jean Verdenal.

The passage is a self-contained narrative that stands out from its surroundings in *Four Quartets* in vivid relief. It opens:

> In the uncertain hour before the morning
> Near the ending of interminable night
> At the recurrent end of the unending
> After the dark dove with the flickering tongue
> Had passed below the horizon of his homing
> While the dead leaves still rattled on like tin

Over the asphalt where no other sound was
  Between three districts whence the smoke arose
  I met one walking, loitering and hurried
As if blown towards me like the metal leaves
  Before the urban dawn wind unresisting.
  And as I fixed upon the down-turned face
That pointed scrutiny with which we challenge
  The first-met stranger in the waning dusk
  I caught the sudden look of some dead master
Whom I had known, forgotten, half recalled
  Both one and many; in the brown baked features
  The eyes of a familiar compound ghost
Both intimate and unidentifiable.
  So I assumed a double part, and cried
  And heard another's voice cry: "What! are *you* here?"

The alert reader familiar with Dante will note echoes of the *Inferno* in this posed question and other details of the passage ("brown baked features"). But Eliot himself has called attention to his use of Dante as a model in a 1950 essay, "What Dante Means to Me": "Twenty years after writing *The Waste Land,* I quote, in *Little Gidding,* a passage which is intended to be the nearest equivalent to a canto of the Inferno or the Purgatorio, in style as well as content, that I could achieve. The intention, of course, was the same as with my allusions to Dante in *The Waste Land:* to present to the mind of the reader a parallel, by means of contrast, between the Inferno and the Purgatorio, which Dante visited and a hallucinated scene after an air-raid. But the method is different: here I was debarred from quoting or adapting at length—I borrowed and adapted freely only a few phrases—because I was *imitating."* [1]

It is of great interest that Eliot linked this "Little Gidding" passage so firmly in his mind with *The Waste Land.* What he does not point out in his comment is that the "few phrases" he did borrow or adapt point to one particular Dante passage, Canto XV of the *Inferno,* "The Violent Against Nature." As in that familiar Canto XXVI of the *Purgatorio* so often quoted by Eliot (and used at the end of *The Waste Land*), Dante and his companion encounter a band of roving sodomites. Among them is the writer Ser Brunetto Latini, who recognizes Dante, pulls at his garment, causing Dante to exclaim, "Ser Brunetto, are *you* here?" The ensuing brief conversation between the two separated friends is a moving one, and Brunetto renders some advice and prognostications for Dante's future. At the end of the canto, Brunetto runs across the plain to rejoin his band of sodomites.

Eliot's interest in this canto dates back to his early work: he refers to it in an important passage of "Tradition and the Individual Talent" (1917) as an example for his "impersonal theory of poetry": "Canto XV of the *Inferno* (Brunetto Latini) is a working up of the emotion evident in the situation; but the effect, though single as that of any work of art, is obtained by considerable complexity of detail. The last quatrain gives an image, a feeling attaching to an image, which 'came,' which did not develop simply out of what precedes, but which was probably in suspension in the poet's mind until the proper combination arrived for it to add itself to."[2] Later, in his 1929 essay "Dante," Eliot provided a prose translation of that final quatrain of Canto XV in which, as Eliot puts it, "Dante dismisses the damned master whom he loves and respects": "Then he turned, and seemed like one of those who runs for the green cloth at Verona through the open field; and of them he seems like him who wins, and not like him who loses." Eliot comments on these lines (in "Dante"): "One does not need to know anything about the race for the roll of green cloth, to be *hit* by these lines; and in making Brunetto, so fallen, *run like the winner,* a quality is given to the punishment which belongs only to the greatest poetry."[3]

Eliot's use of these lines—unquoted—in "Tradition and the Individual Talent," together with his return to them in his "Dante" essay, suggested to one critic that "the Brunetto episode was working obscurely and powerfully on Eliot's imagination."[4] In the context of our discussion of Eliot and Verdenal, particularly as the relationship might have helped in part to shape an essay like "Tradition and the Individual Talent" (see Chapter 4), we might agree with this critic's assessment but reach a conclusion somewhat different from his (that the "compound ghost" of "Little Gidding" was primarily Ezra Pound). Of course, by the very fact of being "compound," a ghost must surely be multiple. And many of the references in the passage do seem to point to Pound: when first encountered he has the "look of some dead master," and in his long speech to the poet he indicates that their common concern had been speech, and "speech impelled" them to "purify the dialect of the tribe." Another critic, Harry Blamires, in *Word Unheard: A Guide Through Eliot's Four Quartets* (1969), has detected many identities in the compound ghost. He lists Dante, Shelley (because of Eliot's discussion of Shelley in "What Dante Means to Me"), Virgil, Shakespeare, Donne, Milton, and others—but not Pound. And he says: "Readers of *In Memoriam* might feel that Tennyson's Hallam, if not Tennyson himself, is now a distinct presence too."[5]

What are the clues that allow so many presences in this "compound ghost"? They tend to be conflicting, but still intriguing. After the posed question, "What! are *you* here?" the poet writes:

> Although we were not. I was still the same,
>   Knowing myself yet being someone other—
>   And he a face still forming; yet the words sufficed
> To compel the recognition they preceded.
>   And so, compliant to the common wind,
>   Too strange to each other for misunderstanding,
> In concord at this intersection time
>   Of meeting nowhere, no before and after,
>   We trod the pavement in a dead patrol.

The recognition appears to be such that the poet and the ghost once knew each other in life and not simply through books. We might even guess that they have experienced Dante together, perhaps even the specific Canto XV of the *Inferno,* because it is Dante's words that "compel" recognition. In the odd encounter, the poet remains the same, but yet he knows himself as "being someone other," and the two are "too strange to each other for misunderstanding." Their acquaintance was long enough in the past to make them "strange" to each other now, with the poet even assuming a "double part"—becoming again his younger self.

The poet is the first to speak: "The wonder that I feel is easy,/ Yet ease is cause to wonder. Therefore speak:/ I may not comprehend, may not remember." The very "ease" the poet feels in the presence of this long-dead friend is cause for "wonder," perhaps because the ghostly presence is familiarly comfortable in memory, however faded in specific outline. Thus it is the poet who bids the ghost speak, recollecting what the poet may not "comprehend," may not "remember." And the ghost recalls their past:

> And he: "I am not eager to rehearse
>   My thought and theory which you have forgotten.
>   These things have served their purpose: let them be.
> So with your own, and pray they be forgiven
>   By others, as I pray you to forgive
>   Both bad and good. Last season's fruit is eaten
> And the fullfed beast shall kick the empty pail.
>   For last year's words belong to last year's language
>   And next year's words await another voice."

These long-ago friends had once had intense literary discussions, perhaps about poetry, perhaps about Dante and others—but these are matters of the past, now gone and forgotten.[6] The pail that held "last-season's fruit" for the "fullfed beast" is now empty, kicked aside and discarded: new fulfillment requires a new pail, another form, a fresh language. The poet's achievements of the past belong to the past, and the future will require "another voice," another poetic identity: much as Eliot's early poetic achievement culminating in *The Waste Land* belonged to his past, and his later achievement, culminating in *Four Quartets,* required a new creation of the poetic self.

These lines on art give way to some fragmentary revelations about the past of the "compound ghost":

> "But, as the passage now presents no hindrance
>   To the spirit unappeased and peregrine
>   Between two worlds become much like each other,
> So I find words I never thought to speak
>   In streets I never thought I should revisit
>   When I left my body on a distant shore."

The speaker characterizes himself as "unappeased" and "peregrine": discontented, disquieted; foreign, coming from abroad. He finds no difficulty in the passage between the two worlds of the *Inferno* (Hell) and twentieth-century bombed-out London because they have become so similar. Thus he is able to speak the words that he never spoke in the place he thought he would never "revisit"—when he left his body "on a distant shore." This last image cannot help but evoke a by now familiar sequence of images from Eliot's pen: "Now lies he there/ Tip to tip washed beneath Charles' Wagon" ("Ode"); "*mort aux Dardanelles*" ("Prufrock" dedication); "the drowned Phoenician Sailor" (*The Waste Land*); "a friend who was later (so far as I could find out) to be mixed with the mud of Gallipoli" (comment in 1934 *Criterion*). These scattered images have their counterpart in *Four Quartets*, particularly in "The Dry Salvages," as in Part IV, "Also pray for those who were in ships, and/ Ended their voyage on the sand, in the sea's lips/ Or in the dark throat which will not reject them/ Or wherever cannot reach them the sound of the sea bell's/ Perpetual angelus."

Surely an important identity of that "compound ghost" is Jean Verdenal, and Eliot's "imitation" of the *Inferno*'s Canto XV, in which he places his long-lost friend in the role of Dante's master Brunetto Latini (roving with his band of sodomites), echoes many previous such associations in Eliot's work, ranging from the reference to "profession of the calamus" in his early "Ode" to his many allusions to the Canto XXVI of the *Purgatorio* ("The Rein of Lust"), as in the quoting of Arnaut Daniel (from the end of Canto XXVI) at the close of *The Waste Land*. It is clearly significant that in the "prophecies" that come at the end of the "compound ghost's" speech, the first has to do with the flesh:

> "Let me disclose the gifts reserved for age
>   To set a crown upon your lifetime's effort.
>   First, the cold friction of expiring sense
> Without enchantment, offering no promise
>   But bitter tastelessness of shadow fruit
>   As body and soul begin to fall asunder.
> Second, the conscious impotence of rage
>   At human folly, and the laceration
>   Of laughter at what ceases to amuse.
> And last, the rending pain of re-enactment
>   Of all that you have done, and been; the shame
>   Of motives late revealed, and the awareness

>   Of things ill done and done to others' harm
>   Which once you took for exercise of virtue.
>   Then fools' approval stings, and honour stains."

This passage seems far removed from matters literary and poetic, and appears to hover on the intimately personal, with elements of remorse and self-accusation. These "gifts reserved for age" are cold gifts indeed. Expiring sense, impotent rage at human folly, shame of self—all add up to an immense futility for the years ahead. Unless, perhaps, they are reminders of the Thunder's voice at the conclusion of *The Waste Land:* Datta, Dayadhvam, Damyata; Give, Sympathize, Control. The "moment's surrender" (Give) of *The Waste Land* becomes but a memory in "expiring sense" in "Little Gidding"; "each in his prison" (Sympathize) becomes the "impotence of rage/ At human folly"; a "heart . . . beating obedient" (Control) becomes shame at "things ill done and done to others' harm."

That peculiar phrase, the "bitter tastelessness of shadow fruit," may refer to the poet's total isolation at the time of the writing of "Little Gidding," 1942: destitute of either friend or wife, or of anyone close, he is reduced in association from the real to its shadow, tasteless indeed. And all the lines devoted to self-shame, with their dark references to "motives late revealed," seem to connect with his treatment of Vivienne, who lived on but was kept from the poet's presence. What he had once taken "for exercise of virtue" he has now come to realize was done for shabby motives. Can it be that there has come a glimmer of awareness of his own responsibility (going all the way back to grief at Verdenal's death) for some of the discord in his life with Vivienne?

The "compound ghost" concludes his discomfiting speech:

>   "From wrong to wrong the exasperated spirit
>   Proceeds, unless restored by that refining fire
>   Where you must move in measure, like a dancer."

As in the three prophecies, this final advice seems to evoke *The Waste Land,* and its conclusion. One of the fragments which the poet-fisher-king uses to shore against his ruins is the line from Canto XXVI of the *Purgatorio,* spoken of Arnaut Daniel: "Then he plunged back into the fire that refines [purifies] them." The poet of *Four Quartets* sees himself as still in need of that "refining fire" of purification. Eliot's "imitation" canto ends:

> The day was breaking. In the disfigured street
>   He left me, with a kind of valediction,
>   And faded on the blowing of the horn.

A valediction, like John Donne's, forbidding mourning? Perhaps. That final "blowing of the horn" is the sounding of the all-clear, after the air raid, bringing the poet out of his fantasy and into his "disfigured street"; and perhaps reminding him of the terrible loss of wars, of the indelible loss at the Dardanelles in World War I, of the random destruction of London (and civilization) in World War II.

13

Making *The Waste Land* Mean

Common teachers or critics are always asking "What does it mean?"
Symphony of fine musician, or sunset, or seawaves rolling up the
beach—what do they mean? Undoubtedly in the most subtle-elusive
sense they mean something—as love does, and religion does, and the
best poem;—but who shall fathom and define those meanings?
                                                        Walt Whitman

Although we have Eliot frequently on record that the critics of *The
Waste Land* were wrong in attributing to him the expression of the
disillusion of a generation, we do not find in any of Eliot's published
prose a firm statement of what he thought he meant in his famous
poem. But of course, in accepting so readily the revisions of Ezra
Pound, Eliot may well have come to feel that the final published
version had already moved considerably from the deeper sources he
knew it to have. Eliot's motives in allowing Pound almost free reign
(not entirely, as we have seen) in slashing the poem might have been
obscure even to himself. He might have recognized that the early
version contained emotion that had been recollected in something less
than genuine tranquility, that his "objective correlative" correlated
more than subjectively with personal experience that must remain
painfully private. And when he said that in *The Waste Land,* "I wasn't
even bothering whether I understood what I was saying,"[1] he thought
that the original manuscript was lost and that the published version
was all that remained for discovering his original meaning.

   Ezra Pound, of course, knew *The Waste Land* in both its manuscript
and published versions.[2] What did he think the poem meant? He
was generally silent on the poem, as he was on the meanings of his

own poetry, but he made a few remarks from which we might make
some intelligent guesses. In reply to a reviewer who had charged *The
Waste Land* with obscurity, Pound wrote in 1924: "I saw the poem in
typescript, and I did not see the notes till 6 or 8 months afterward;
and they have not increased my enjoyment of the poem one atom.
The poem seems to me an emotional unit."[3] Of course, the poem
Pound saw in typescript was far different from the poem that was
published, but his view of the notes is close in spirit to Eliot's later
repudiation of them. Still, even in his repudiation, Eliot reaffirmed
his need to acknowledge Jessie Weston's *From Ritual to Romance* as a
primary source. Pound said, however: "I have not read Miss
Weston's *Ritual to Romance,* and do not at present intend to. As to the
citations, I do not think it matters a damn which is from Day, which
from Milton, Middleton, Webster, or Augustine. I mean so far as the
functioning of the poem is concerned. One's incult pleasure in reading *The Waste Land* would be the same if Webster had written
'Women Before Woman' and Marvell the *Metamorphoses.*" Perhaps.
But the question that remains unanswered is the question of the
original context of the quotations. It may matter little whether Ovid
or Marvell wrote the *Metamorphoses,* but it seems to matter a good
deal (often, if not always) whether the reader knows a borrowed
quotation in the context of its source—as *The Waste Land* takes on
meaning from the unseen as well as the seen.

Pound's irritation with *The Waste Land*'s early detractors elicited
this comment on the obsessive search for meaning: "This demand
for clarity in every particular of a work, whether essential or not,
reminds me of the Pre-Raphaelite painter who was doing a twilight
scene but rowed across the river in day time to see the shape of the
leaves on the further bank, which he then drew in with full detail."
The example Pound cites is seductive, but the gist of his remark is
perhaps more revealing than he intended. It might even be a confession that he himself did not find "clarity in every particular" of *The
Waste Land* and, moreover, was careless of such clarity when he
revised the poem. It is of some interest that not once did Pound, in
his revision, say that a particular scene or passage was essential but
needed re-imagining or re-seeing. His revision was actually a drastic
cutting. It was as though he made up his mind that the only unity in
the poem was emotional ("The poem seems to me an emotional

unit"), and it could therefore sustain any amount of cutting, and needed no major rewriting. But of course he was adamant, when Eliot queried him on the few remaining lines of the slashed Part IV, that Phlebas the Phoenician remain in the poem because he was introduced by the Tarot cards and was an "integral part of the poem." It seems as though, by this time, Pound had a vision of *The Waste Land* that Eliot no longer understood or shared; Eliot felt a loss of meaning, while Pound sensed the development of a new meaning that Eliot had not foreseen.

Some notion of what Pound seemed to see as the significance of *The Waste Land* may be found in a 1922 letter to Felix Schelling.[4] It is a long letter primarily justifying, explaining, and defending his own work. That Pound mentions the still unpublished *Waste Land* at all comes as something of a surprise—almost as though he considered it part of his own production. His mention of Eliot's poem comes in a passage in defense of didacticism: "I am perhaps didactic; so in a sense, or in different senses are Homer, Dante, Villon, and Omar, and Fitzgerald's trans. of Omar is the only good poem of Vict. era that has got beyond a fame de cénacle. It's all rubbish to pretend that art isn't didactic. A revelation is always didactic. Only the aesthetes since 1880 have pretended the contrary, and they aren't a very sturdy lot." Omar Khayyám was one of Pound's genuine weaknesses, a bizarre taste for one who shaped the modernity of modern poetry! But there it is, like Eliot's liking for Kipling. Pound goes on: "Art can't offer a patent medicine. A failure to dissociate that from a profounder didacticism has led to the errors of 'aesthete's' critique."

What is the nature of this "profounder didacticism" that has led to Pound's extended defense, and then to a mention of Eliot? Pound began this section of his letter annoyed by a phrase his correspondent had somehow applied to Pound's poetry: "Next point: This being buoyed by wit. No. *Punch* and the rest of them have too long gone on treating the foetor of England as if it were something to be joked about. There is an evil without dignity and without tragedy, and it is dishonest art to treat it as if it were funny. It is perhaps difficult to treat it at all; the Brit. Empire is rotting because no one in England tries to treat it. Juvenal isn't witty. Joyce's isn't harsh enough. One hasn't any theology to fall back on." Clearly a raw nerve has been touched in Pound, and he comes back some paragraphs later to make his point with more venom: "My main objection is to your phrase about being buoyed by wit. If the poets don't make certain horrors appear horrible who will? (This arrogance is not mine but Shelley's, and it is absolutely true. Humanity is malleable mud, and the arts set the moulds it is later cast into. Until the cells of humanity recognize certain things as excrement, they will stay in [the] human colon and poison it. Victoria was an excrement, Curtis Lorrimer, *all* British journalism are excrement. Bottomley has been jailed and Northcliffe gone off his head to prove this.)"

It is surely significant that, sandwiched between these two outbursts, in the midst of a long defense of his own work, Pound casually remarks: "Eliot's *Waste Land* is I think the justification of the 'movement,' of our modern experiment, since 1900. It shd. be published this year." It is not unreasonable to conclude that Pound found *The Waste Land,* as he had so drastically revised it, filled with the kind of "profounder didacticism" that he describes in the above passages. Indeed, it is not too venturesome to conclude that Pound cut out the passages that did not contribute to that didacticism, and sharpened the didacticism of the passages that remained by remarkable pruning. Pound thus turned a somewhat personal, confessional poem into a public, didactic poem with the assistance of an author who was filled with uncertainties about the personal-confessional content to begin with. As that content receded, Eliot became more bewildered about his own meaning, and never conceded that the meaning that Pound shaped in revising the poem was ever a part of his original intention, repeatedly insisting in later life that *The Waste Land* was not a "criticism of the contemporary world."

But of course the most persistent reading of *The Waste Land* is precisely that it is a *devastating* criticism of the modern world. This interpretation was established early in the reviews of the poem, and endures vigorously today. One of the most distinguished critics who set this direction in the criticism is Edmund Wilson. His review appeared in December 1922, in the *Dial,* and was later revised and published in *Axel's Castle* (1931). It is curious that Wilson sensed but did not explore very deeply the personal or idiosyncratic aspect of the consciousness behind the poem, but dismissed it as Puritanism: "We recognize throughout *The Waste Land* the peculiar conflicts of the Puritan turned artist: the horror of vulgarity and the shy sym-

pathy with the common life, the ascetic shrinking from sexual experience and the distress at the drying up of the springs of sexual
emotion, with the straining after a religious emotion which may be
made to take its place."[5] But Wilson moved away from this direction
quickly to point the way for future social critics: "The terrible dreariness of the great modern cities is the atmosphere in which *The Waste
Land* takes place—amidst this dreariness, brief, vivid images emerge,
brief pure moments of feeling are distilled; but all about us we are
aware of nameless millions performing barren office routines, wear-
ing down their souls in interminable labours of which the products
never bring them profit—people whose pleasures are so sordid and
so feeble that they seem almost sadder than their pains." The social
criticism in this passage is verging on the sociological or political;
note in the passage which follows how easily Wilson slides from the
poem's view of the world to his and his reader's ("we"): "And this
Waste Land has another aspect: it is a place not merely of desolation,
but of anarchy and doubt. In our post-War world of shattered insti-
tutions, strained nerves and bankrupt ideals, life no longer seems
serious or coherent—we have no belief in the things we do and
consequently we have no heart for them." Wilson has by now left the
Puritan consciousness of the poem far behind, and has discovered
instead a universal consciousness identical with his own.

In direct contrast with Edmund Wilson, I.A. Richards emphasized
in his reading of *The Waste Land* the absence of any kind of systematic statement—about the world or anything else. In a comment
that Eliot himself called into question (in *The Use of Poetry and the Use
of Criticism*, 1933), Richards found that *The Waste Land* effected "a
complete severance between poetry and *all* beliefs."[6] Richards provided some explanation of what he meant in an appendix to a second edition of *Principles of Literary Criticism* (1926). Richards traced
the "bewilderment" which Eliot's poetry caused to "the unobtrusive-
ness, in some cases the absence, of any coherent intellectual thread
upon which the items of the poem are strung." The "items," Richards asserted, were united "by the accord, contrast, and interaction
of their emotional effects, not by an intellectual scheme that analysis
must work out." Thus, Richards found, any unity must be located in
the "unified response which this interaction creates in the right
reader. The only intellectual activity required takes place in the

realisation of the separate items." If the reader works out a "ratio-nalisation" of his experience in reading the poem, he is "adding something that does not belong to the poem." Richards provided a name for the technique Eliot used in *The Waste Land:* "a 'music of ideas.' The ideas are of all kinds: abstract and concrete, general and particular; and, like the musician's phrases, they are arranged, not that they may tell us something, but that their effects in us may combine into a coherent whole of feeling and attitude and produce a peculiar liberation of the will." Richards' approach to *The Waste Land* through its techniques enables him to assert: "Mr. Eliot is neither sighing after vanished glories nor holding contemporary experience up to scorn." This must have been news to many readers of the poem, including Edmund Wilson. In concluding, Richards empha-sized that the technique of the poem was such as to enable its nega-tivism to generate a kind of final affirmation: "Both bitterness and desolation are superficial aspects of his [Eliot's] poetry. There are those who think that he merely takes his readers into the *Waste Land* and leaves them there, that in his last poem he confesses his impo-tence to release the healing waters. The reply is that some readers find in his poetry not only a clearer, fuller realisation of their plight, the plight of a whole generation, than they find elsewhere, but also through the very energies set free in that realisation a return of the saving passion."[7] It was that phrase, "plight of a whole generation," that Eliot was to disavow repeatedly later in trying to straighten the crooked path criticism of his poem had taken.

Edmund Wilson and I.A. Richards provided, in their early criti-cism of *The Waste Land,* the basic directions that later, more elaborate commentaries would take. There is no need here to follow in detail the interpretive history of the poem (however interesting that might in itself prove). But I would like to look briefly at two additional commentaries. F.R. Leavis was concerned, in *New Bearings in English Poetry* (1932), in defining the obscure unity of the poem, and seems to have borrowed in part from I.A. Richards: "The unity of *The Waste Land* is no more 'metaphysical' than it is narrative or dramatic, and to try to elucidate it metaphysically reveals complete misunder-standing. The unity the poem aims at is that of an inclusive con-sciousness: the organization it achieves as a work of art is the kind that has been illustrated, an organization that may, by analogy, be called musical." Since the poem's unity is not metaphysical, narrative, or dramatic, but musical, it does not portray change: "It exhibits no progression: 'I sat upon the shore/ Fishing, with the arid plain behind me.'—the thunder brings no rain to revive the Waste Land, and the poem ends where it began."[8]

Cleanth Brooks, in his 1939 reading of *The Waste Land*, specifically disavowed this F.R. Leavis position, asserting that there was indeed progression in the poem: "The comment upon what the thunder says would indicate, if other passages did not, that the poem does 'not end where it began.'" The point is important, because it is the "progression" that Brooks discovered in the poem that enabled him to conclude that *The Waste Land* is, ultimately, an affirmation of religious belief. Thus he stated that *The Waste Land* "has been almost consistently misinterpreted since its first publication. Even a critic so acute as Edmund Wilson has seen the poem as essentially a statement of despair and disillusionment, and his account sums up the stock interpretation of the poem. Indeed, the phrase, 'the poetry of drouth', has become a cliché of left-wing criticism." Thus, emphatically, *The Waste Land* "is not a world-weary cry of despair or a sighing after the vanished glories of the past."[9]

Brooks was confident enough of the poem's meaning to commit it to explicit statement: "Eliot's theme is the rehabilitation of a system of beliefs, known but now discredited." Because these beliefs are discredited, Eliot could not make a direct approach (as did Dante), but he had to "work by indirection" in order to get read at all: "The Christian material is at the center, but the poet never deals with it directly. The theme of resurrection is made on the surface in terms of the fertility rites; the words which the thunder speaks are Sanscrit words." In his conclusion, Brooks appears to push his summary somewhat beyond the support generated by the details of his analysis: "To put the matter in still other terms: the Christian terminology is for the poet a mass of clichés. However 'true' he may feel the terms to be, he is still sensitive to the fact that they operate superficially as clichés, and his method of necessity must be a process of bringing them to life again. The method adopted in *The Waste Land* is thus violent and radical, but thoroughly necessary. For the renewing and vitalizing of symbols which have been crusted over with a distorting familiarity demands the type of organization which we have already commented on."[10] The fervor that comes through the affirmations may strike many (or some) as that of the believer who is finding confirmation of his belief as much in his own intensity as in the place he gazes.

But *The Waste Land* has seemed to be from the beginning a kind of incredibly complicated ink blot designed for a Rorschach test, confirming whatever is already present in the eye of the beholder. Whether Marxist, Christian, or merely aesthete, readers could hail the poem as summing up the attitude of a generation. And the poem's "meaning" became embodied not only in criticism, sociology, and history, but also in other works of art. Take, for example, three American novels: F. Scott Fitzgerald's *The Great Gatsby* (1925) presents a waste land in miniature in the valley of ashes that lies between West Egg and New York; Ernest Hemingway's *The Sun Also Rises* (1926) presents an impotent hero as spokesman for a lost generation living meaningless lives; William Faulkner's *Sanctuary* (1931) presents still other impotent (both psychically and physically) characters living and dying in a world of purposeless, pointless violence. These are but three instances that could be multiplied endlessly of works directly or indirectly influenced by *The Waste Land*—and the very influence suggesting an interpretation of the poem.

Thus making *The Waste Land* mean has been a task pursued with determination over a half-century by critics, poets, and novelists, with a conspicuous lack of unanimity as to what that meaning is— and with the bemused dismay of the poem's author. It would be difficult to find in all literary history a poet whose poem appeared abandoned so completely to others for revision and interpretation. It is almost as though it were snatched from the author's hands and cut, shaped, and read to fit the needs of an ailing modern age. And before his very eyes, his poem was metamorphosed into another identity, another existence, with which he himself would eventually need to come to terms.

14

Letting *The Waste Land* Be

The chief use of the "meaning of a poem," in the ordinary sense, may be ... to satisfy one habit of the reader, to keep his mind diverted and quiet, while the poem does its work upon him. ...

                                                              T.S. Eliot

All of the diversity of interpretive opinion on *The Waste Land* was something that Eliot himself was acutely aware of, and which clearly changed the way he looked at poetry, and his own poetry in particular. In *The Use of Poetry and the Use of Criticism* (1933) Eliot discussed at some length I.A. Richards' views of *The Waste Land,* but in an interesting passage he disavowed any special authority on his own poem: "There are two reasons why the writer of poetry must not be thought to have any great advantage. One is that a discussion of poetry such as this takes us far outside the limits within which a poet may speak with authority; the other is that the poet does many things upon instinct, for which he can give no better account than anybody else." The poet may report how he writes, and if he is honest the report may be useful. Eliot then adds a comment that seems by its nature to apply to his own experience with *The Waste Land*: "In one sense, but a very limited sense, he [the poet] knows better what his poems 'mean' than anyone else; he may know the history of their composition, the material which has gone in and come out in an unrecognisable form, and he knows what he was trying to do and what he was meaning to mean" (pp. 129–30).

Eliot seems hovering at the edge, here, of telling us that the material that went into *The Waste Land* came out in such an "unrecognisable form" that no one had seen or witnessed its presence; and that

even "what he was meaning to mean" in *The Waste Land* had remained undetected by the critics. He goes on immediately to say:
"But what a poem means is as much what it means to others as what
it means to the author; and indeed, in the course of time a poet may
become merely a reader in respect to his own works, forgetting his
original meaning—or without forgetting, merely changing" (p. 130).
Eliot turns at once to a critic's comments on *The Waste Land,* hinting
strongly that his own experience with that poem was what lay behind
the somewhat startling generalization. In short, Eliot seems to be
saying indirectly that not only have the critics failed to find what he
meant to mean in *The Waste Land,* but that he is ready to concede
that the meaning that they have found is, indeed, the (or *a*) meaning
of the poem, as he has become "merely a reader in respect to his
own works." In becoming such a reader, the author may be in the
position of simply "forgetting his original meaning." But Eliot adds a
significant dash at this point, surely to cover his own case—"or without forgetting, merely changing." These remarks were made in
1933, and it was the very next year that Eliot broke through the
review formula of his commentary in *The Criterion* with the poignant
outburst about Jean Verdenal ("the memory of a friend coming
across the Luxembourg Gardens in the late afternoon, waving a
branch of lilac"). Eliot had not in 1933 forgotten the materials that
had gone into his poem, nor what he had meant to mean—but he
had, perhaps, changed: reconciled to a reading of the poem that was
totally unaware of its personal dimension.

And of course, Eliot in a sense is right: poems mean what readers
take them to mean. And readers have frequently surprised authors
by finding meanings the author did not appear to have in mind. But
Eliot's strategy in his 1933 lectures, after granting the readers their
right to their meaning, was to find meaning less than central to the
experiencing of poetry: "The chief use of the 'meaning' of a poem,
in the ordinary sense, may be (for here again I am speaking of some
kinds of poetry and not all) to satisfy one habit of the reader, to keep
his mind diverted and quiet, while the poem does its work upon
him: much as the imaginary burglar is always provided with a bit of
nice meat for the house-dog. This is a normal situation of which I
approve. But the minds of all poets do not work that way; some of
them, assuming that there are other minds like their own, become

impatient of this 'meaning' which seems superfluous, and perceive possibilities of intensity through its elimination."[1]

If we take this passage as an indirect reference to *The Waste Land* (and I think we may), Eliot seems to be having his revenge on all those who have provided their own "meaning" for the poem. It is surely significant that Eliot places the key word of his comment, "meaning," in quotation marks. What indeed is the meaning of the "meaning" of a poem, especially if the poem has work to do while its "meaning" provides simply a diversion, a deflection of attention. It is clear that the "meaning" Eliot has reference to is that public statement or social criticism which so many critics had discussed and analyzed in *The Waste Land*—which in effect they had made *The Waste Land* "mean." But the "work" *The Waste Land* "does" on the reader while his attention (or rational faculty) is chasing after the public "meaning" is surely on the private feelings below the levels of consciousness—engaging the emotions so powerfully (and covertly) dramatized in the poem, those very feelings of loss and pain and anguish, of "memory and desire," that we have been tracing through the poem. Thus Eliot's advice seems to be that as readers we must become less intellectually aggressive and more emotionally accessible, especially on the lower levels of consciousness. Instead of making *The Waste Land* mean, we must let *The Waste Land* be—so that it might do its proper "work" upon us.

In these comments about "meaning," Eliot seems to be getting close to a theory that he would develop more fully later, in "The Three Voices of Poetry" (1953), especially in his description of the first voice—the voice of the poet talking to himself. This kind of poetry seems to render "meaning" almost irrelevant: "What you start from is nothing so definite as an emotion, in any ordinary sense; it is still more certainly not an idea. . . . In a poem which is neither didactic nor narrative, and not animated by any other social purpose, the poet may be concerned solely with expressing in verse—using all his resources of words, with their history, their connotations, their music—this obscure impulse."[2] Although such poetry may be written to exorcise a demon, or to "gain relief from acute discomfort," Eliot insists that the biographical data lying behind the poem will lead away from rather than into the poem. It is at this point that Eliot appears to be addressing John Peter and his *Waste Land* interpretation suppressed by Eliot's solicitors: "The attempt to explain the poem by tracing it back to its origins will distract attention from the poem, to direct it on to something else which, in the form in which it can be apprehended by the critic and his readers, has no relation to the poem and throws no light upon it."[3]

In the form in which it can be apprehended by the critic and his readers. We paused over this phrase in Chapter 4. Perhaps now we can explore its implication in a little more depth. In our speculative tracing of *The Waste Land* back to its origins, the "something else" (something other than the poem) to which we have directed our attention is the biographical information concerning Eliot's early relation to Jean Verdenal and his later relation to his wife Vivienne. This "tracing" has been largely confined to the first three chapters of the book. All the remainder has concentrated attention on Eliot's work, with Chapters 6 to 10 constituting a systematic look at *The Waste Land* itself. In short, we have not used the work to reconstruct the life, but have rather used the life to illuminate the work. Thus, we have not deflected attention from the poem but, on the contrary, have deepened interest in the poem's obscurities and ambiguities.

Moreover, we have not been reductive with the biographical data, diminishing them to the grossest possible terms to exploit their potential for sensationalism. What actually happened, if anything, between Eliot and Verdenal has not been of primary concern here: rather, Eliot's imaginative transfiguration of the relationship in the shaping of his poetry has been the focus of attention. As I indicated at the opening of Chapter 6, we need know nothing whatever of Jean Verdenal in order to read *The Waste Land* in the way we have read it. And indeed, we may attribute to Eliot's imagination the entire emotional content of the relationship—that would have been sufficient, together with the emotionally related elements, to inspire the poem: sufficient, that is, for a man of Eliot's poetic genius. It is surely obvious that such relationships, real or imagined, cannot be the primary "cause" for great poetry: there must be first the "individual talent."

No doubt Eliot's fear that the critic and his readers, in tracing back to its origins such a poem as *The Waste Land,* could not "apprehend" in its authentic "form" the basic biographical elements, had justification. What is beyond "apprehension" is the imaginative metamorphoses these elements undergo in their complicated progress from fact to poetry. To reduce the poetry back to the fact is, of course, horrendously distortive. My intention has been to remain sensitive to Eliot's admonition throughout, guarding against the reduction of the poetry to biography, but attempting always to see the ways the biography was transfigured and diffused in the poetry. In short, I have tried to "apprehend" the origins of *The Waste Land* with some of the imaginative intensity with which Eliot himself apprehended them, moving not back to the fact or event, but always forward to poetic image and expression.

With all this in mind, it is something of a shock to come upon such a reference as Frank Kermode's (see Chapter 2, note 12) to "the homosexual interpretation of *The Waste Land*." Such a phrase does indeed justify Eliot's fears about critics delving into poetic origins. But such a phrase is, too, highly reductive, implying that "the heterosexual interpretation of *The Waste Land*" (patently absurd) was the only feasible one. The ludicrous ineptness of such phrases might be suggested by characterizing *Romeo and Juliet* as a story of the repercussions of juvenile premarital sex, or *Ulysses* as a story of an adulterous, oversexed wife, or *The Scarlet Letter* as the story of a promiscuous puritan and her sexual affairs. Such characterizations are not only reductive but destructive, not to say simple-minded. All of these works are made up of complex patterns of human feelings and psychology, emotions and thoughts; to reduce any one of them to a one-dimensional sexual characterization is to falsify or sensationalize.

How does our awareness of the poem's origins—and especially of how those origins have become embedded in the final version— affect our reading of a poem called *The Waste Land* published in 1922 and still going by that name today? Each reader must answer that question for himself, of course. And it will be the rare reader who does not feel that Pound, whatever his view of the poem's meaning, in some sense improved it by his pruning and cutting: sharpening its images, deepening its intensities, modulating its movements, highlighting its contrasts—while, at the same time, obscuring its origins. It would be pointless to quarrel with the established version of *The Waste Land,* to which Pound's almost impeccable judgment contributed so much—just as it is pointless to reject Whitman's deathbed edition of *Leaves of Grass,* so radically altered by the older poet from the shocking 1855 visionary version of *Leaves*. And yet, as we find Whitman's earlier *Leaves* illuminating his later version, so we may find Eliot's original *Waste Land* clarifying the final form.

However comfortably accustomed to reading *The Waste Land* the reader has become, there are likely to be opaque passages that my commentary and exploration will illuminate or clarify. Thus guided we might read the "final" version of *The Waste Land* with more understanding, regardless of our established approach. But more than this, familiarity with the way the poem came into being should provide another dimension to the experience of the poem, a dimension that need not, for its own validity, supplant other possibilities of meaning. In my explorations of the poem's origins and evolution, its beginnings and growth—and its final shaping by those original impulses—I have sensed its resonance deepening, its texture intensifying in complexity and richness. It is my hope that the reader will share my experience in his exploration of T.S. Eliot's personal *Waste Land*.

Perhaps the most enduring and profound effect this exploration could have on reading *The Waste Land* is to reinforce the advice implicit in one statement after another from the poet himself: stop making *The Waste Land* mean; start letting *The Waste Land* be.

Notes

I have given sufficient data in the text for readers to locate Eliot's own lines of poetry or his notes in *The Waste Land* (1922 version) or in *The Waste Land: A Facsimile* (1971).

Preface

1. *Selected Essays: New Edition* (New York: Harcourt, Brace, 1950), p. 7.
2. *On Poetry and Poets* (London: Faber and Faber, 1957; rpt. New York, Noonday-Farrar, Straus, & Giroux, 1961), p. 124.
3. See the letter from Peter du Sautoy of Faber and Faber to *The New York Review of Books* 23, no. 6 (15 April 1976), p. 40: "In a Memorandum dated September 30th 1963, attached to his will (not in the will itself), T.S. Eliot wrote: 'I do not wish my Executors to facilitate or countenance the writing of any biography of me.' "
4. *To Criticize the Critic* (New York: Farrar, Straus & Giroux, 1965). See especially pp. 15–20.
5. Quotations from Ellmann cited in the text are from *Golden Codgers: Biographical Speculations* (London: Oxford University Press, 1973).
6. *The Use of Poetry and the Use of Criticism* (New York: Barnes & Noble, 1933), p. 130.

1. Prologue: A Curious Shudder

1. Page numbers in the text refer to *Selected Essays* (1950).

2. An Interpretation Suppressed: Amazement and Disgust

1. *The Waste Land: A Facsimile and Transcript of the Original Drafts,* ed. Valerie Eliot (New York: Harcourt Brace Jovanovich, 1971), p. 1.
2. *Selected Essays* (1950), p. 324.
3. George Plimpton, ed., *Writers at Work: The Paris Review Interviews (Second Series)* (New York: Viking Press, 1963), pp. 97, 105.
4. *The Use of Poetry and the Use of Criticism,* p. 130.
5. *On Poetry and Poets,* p. 137. A valuable listing of Eliot's comments on *The Waste Land* may be found in Leonard Unger, "T.S.E. on *The Waste Land*," *Mosaic* 6 (Fall 1972): 157–65.
6. *T.S. Eliot: A Memoir* (New York: Dodd, Mead, 1971), p. 243.
7. "A New Interpretation of *The Waste Land*," *Essays in Criticism* 2 (July 1952): 245.
8. "Postscript," *Essays in Criticism* 19 (April 1969): 165–66.
9. C.B. Cox and Arnold P. Hinchcliffe, *T.S. Eliot, The Waste Land: A Casebook* (New York: Macmillan, 1968), p. 16.

10. London *Times Literary Supplement,* 14 January 1972, p. 3646. G. Wilson Knight elaborated his views in "Thoughts on *The Waste Land,*" *The Denver Quarterly* 7, no. 2 (Summer 1972): 1–13.

11. See "The Letters Column," *Times Literary Supplement* for 21, 28 January; 4, 11, 18, 25 February; 3 March 1972.

12. Review of *The Waste Land: A Facsimile, Atlantic Monthly* 229 (January 1972): 90.

3. Faint Clews and Indirections: The Sub-Surface Life

1. "A Commentary," *The Criterion* 13 (April 1934): 452.

2. *Eliot and His Age* (New York: Random House, 1971), p. 33; *T.S. Eliot* (New York: Macmillan, 1972), p. 10.

3. *T.S. Eliot: A Memoir,* p. 32; *Great Tom: Notes Toward a Definition of T.S. Eliot* (New York: Harper & Row, 1974), pp. 33–34.

4. George Watson, "Quest for a Frenchman," *Sewanee Review* 84 (Summer 1976): 466–75.

5. *The Waste Land: A Facsimile,* p. ix.

6. Russell's quotations cited in the text are from *The Autobiography: 1914–1944* (Boston: Little, Brown, 1968).

7. *The Waste Land: A Facsimile,* p. xxii.

8. Ibid., p. 129.

9. *Eliot and His Age,* p. 39.

10. *T.S. Eliot,* p. 32.

11. *T.S. Eliot: A Memoir,* p. 55.

12. *Great Tom,* pp. 43–45.

13. "T.S. Eliot: The Psychobiographical Approach," *Southern Review* 6 (March 1973): 21.

14. "T.S. Eliot and *The Waste Land:* Psychopathological Antecedents and Transformations," *Archives of General Psychiatry* 30 (May 1974): 709, 712.

15. *The Autobiography,* p. 9.

16. *Selected Essays* (1950), pp. 234–35. I am indebted to John Peter's "Postscript" to his "A New Interpretation of *The Waste Land*" for calling attention to this Eliot passage.

17. F. Scott Fitzgerald, *The Crack-Up,* ed. Edmund Wilson (New York: New Directions, 1945), p. 310.

18. *The Great Gatsby* (New York: Charles Scribner's Sons, 1925); rpt. paperback, pp. 97, 182.

19. T.S. Eliot, "Introduction," *Nightwood,* by Djuna Barnes (New York: Harcourt, Brace, 1937; rpt. New York: New Directions Paperbook No. 98, 1961), pp. xi–xvi.

20. *The Waste Land: A Facsimile,* pp. 91–93.

4. Critical Theory: Escaping Personality—Exorcising Demons

1. *On Poetry and Poets,* p. 117.

2. *To Criticize the Critic and Other Writings,* p. 17.

3. Ibid., p. 19.

4. *The Waste Land: A Facsimile,* p. x.

5. Ibid., pp. xi, xiii.

6. *Selected Essays* (1950), pp. 7, 10, 11.

7. Ibid, pp. 124–25.

8. Ibid., p. 247.

9. *The Sacred Wood* (London: Methuen, 1928; rpt. The Fountain Library, 1934), pp. vii, ix–x.

10. See especially John Peter's "Postscript" (pp. 170–71) to his "A New Reading of *The Waste Land*" for a cataloguing of all Eliot's references to Canto XXVI of Dante's *Purgatorio.*

11. *On Poetry and Poets,* p. 107.

12. Plimpton, *Writers at Work (Second Series),* p. 105.

13. *On Poetry and Poets,* pp. 107–8.

14. Ibid., p. 123.

15. "Fifty Years of American Poetry," *The Third Book of Criticism* (New York: Farrar, Straus & Giroux, 1969), pp. 314–15.

5. *A Suppressed "Ode": Confessional Poem*

1. For descriptions of the two volumes discussed here, see Donald Gallup, *T.S. Eliot: A Bibliography* (New York: Harcourt, Brace & World, 1969), pp. 25–27.

2. Donald Gallup, "The 'Lost' Manuscripts of T.S. Eliot," *Times Literary Supplement,* 7 November 1968, p. 1240.

3. *Ara Vos Prec* (London: Ovid Press, 1920), p. 30.

4. Sydney Musgrove, *T.S. Eliot and Walt Whitman* (Wellington: New Zealand University Press, 1952).

5. Gallup, "The 'Lost' Manuscripts of T.S. Eliot," p. 1240.

6. Kristian Smidt, *Poetry and Belief in the Work of T.S. Eliot,* rev. ed. (London: Routledge and Kegan Paul, 1961), p. 85.

7. Gaius Valerius Catullus, Poem #61: "You Who Dwell upon Helicon," tr. L.R. Lind, *Latin Poetry* (Boston: Houghton Mifflin, 1957), p. 43.

8. Ovid, *Metamorphoses,* tr. Rolfe Humphries (Bloomington: Indiana University Press, 1961), p. 109.

6. *Memory and Desire: "Burial of the Dead"*

1. *The Waste Land: A Facsimile,* pp. x, xviii, xviii.

2. Ibid, p. xxi.

3. See accounts by Grover Smith, "The Making of *The Waste Land*," *Mosaic* 6 (Fall 1972): 127–41; and Hugh Kenner, "The Urban Apocalypse," *Eliot in His Time,* ed. A. Walton Litz (Princeton: Princeton University Press, 1973), pp. 23–49.

4. See Hugh Kenner, *The Invisible Poet: T.S. Eliot* (New York: Harcourt,

Brace & World, 1959), pp. 147–51.

5. D.D. Paige, ed., *The Letters of Ezra Pound: 1907–1941* (New York: Harcourt, Brace & World, 1950), p. 171.

6. *On Poetry and Poets*, pp. 121–22.

7. *The Waste Land: A Facsimile*, p. xxii.

8. See Valerie Eliot's note, *The Waste Land: A Facsimile*, p. 125.

9. *The Letters of Ezra Pound*, p. 171.

10. George L.K. Morris, "Marie, Marie, Hold on Tight," *T.S. Eliot: A Collection of Critical Essays*, ed. Hugh Kenner (Englewood Cliffs, N.J.: Prentice-Hall, 1962), pp. 86–88.

11. *The Waste Land: A Facsimile*, p. 126.

12. Ibid, p. 129.

13. *Poems Written in Early Youth* (New York: Farrar, Straus & Giroux, 1967), pp. 28–30. This "corrected" version has been quoted here.

14. *T.S. Eliot's Poetry and Plays: A Study in Sources and Meaning* (Chicago: University of Chicago Press, 1956), pp. 74–75.

15. *Metamorphoses*, tr. Rolfe Humphries, p. 240.

16. See *The Ghost Sonata* in *Six Plays of Strindberg*, tr. Elizabeth Sprigge (New York: Doubleday Anchor Books, 1955), pp. 295–304.

17. G. Wilson Knight, "Thoughts on *The Waste Land*," p. 3. For a similar conjecture, see John Peter, "A New Interpretation of *The Waste Land*."

18. See Barbara Everett, "Eliot in and out of *The Waste Land*," *Critical Quarterly* 17, no. 1 (Spring 1975): 17.

7. In the Cage: "A Game of Chess"

1. *The Waste Land: A Facsimile*, pp. 104–7.

2. Ibid., pp. 118–21.

3. Louis Simpson, *Three on the Tower* (New York: William Morrow, 1975), p. 144.

4. *The Waste Land: A Facsimile*, p. 126.

8. In Rats' Alley: "The Fire Sermon"

1. Henry Clarke Warren, *Buddhism in Translations* (Cambridge: Harvard University Press, 1896; rpt. 1953), p. 353.

2. Plimpton, *Writers at Work (Second Series)*, p. 96.

3. *The Waste Land: A Facsimile*, p. 127.

4. See Russell on Vivienne as discussed in Chapter 3.

5. *On Poetry and Poets*, p. 122.

6. For example, see Cleanth Brooks, "*The Waste Land*: Critique of the Myth," reprinted in *T.S. Eliot, The Waste Land: A Casebook*, pp. 128–61.

7. *From Ritual to Romance* (New York: Doubleday Anchor Books, 1957), p. 23.

8. See especially Harry Trosman, "T.S. Eliot and *The Waste Land.*"

9. Trosman sees Eliot's father's death in 1919 of "paramount importance." I would not want to minimize it, but it seems clear to me that Eliot's primary linkages of the Shakespearean line are with the drowned sailor and the hyacinth garden, and thus with Verdenal. See also the last fragment of *The Waste Land: A Facsimile and Transcript,* untitled, which opens "Those are pearls that were his eyes," and closes: "Still and quiet brother are you still and quiet." Also see discussions of "brother" references in Chapters 9 and 10 (section on lines 395–422).

10. See Smith, *T.S. Eliot's Poetry and Plays,* p. 86.

11. *The Creative Experiment* (London: Macmillan, 1967), p. 182.

12. *Oeuvres Poétiques Complètes* (Paris: Éditions Vialetay, 1955), III, 44: " . . . et sa pente/ Vers la Chair de garcon vierge que cela tente/ D'aimer les seins légers et ce gentil babil."

13. *Metamorphoses,* p. 67.

14. "A New Interpretation of *The Waste Land,*" p. 259.

15. *The Confessions of St. Augustine,* tr. E.B. Pusey (New York: Dutton, 1942), Book IV, Paragraph 9, pp. 56, 58.

9. Suffering a Sea-Change: "Death by Water"

1. *The Letters of Ezra Pound,* p. 171.

2. *The Waste Land: A Facsimile,* p. 128.

3. Ibid., pp. 118–21.

4. Ibid., pp. 122–23.

5. *The Complete Poems and Plays: 1909–1950* (New York: Harcourt, Brace, 1950), pp. 31–32. My translation.

6. *Selected Essays* (1950), p. 233: "The type of sexual experience which Dante describes as occurring to him at the age of nine years is by no means impossible or unique. My only doubt (in which I found myself confirmed by a distinguished psychologist) is whether it could have taken place so *late* in life as the age of nine years. The psychologist agreed with me that it is more likely to occur at about five or six years of age."

7. *A Reader's Guide to T.S. Eliot* (New York: Noonday Press, 1953), pp. 115–18.

8. See Grover Smith, "Observations on Eliot's 'Death by Water,'" *Accent* 6 (Summer 1946): 257–63, for earlier speculation on the sexual connotations of the section and on the possible connection of Phlebas with Mr. Eugenides. Especially interesting are Smith's comments on the origins of the word *phlebas* (p. 260): "The meaning of the name Phlebas, by which the Phoenician is known in 'Death by Water,' is derived, I am disposed to think, from the Greek *phlép: phlebós,* a vein. This would fit very well with the common expression 'vein of commerce' in connection with the Phoenician's role as a trader. But even more remarkable is the fact that the Greek word has another meaning, which is the same as that of *phallós*—a most rewarding fact, if it confirms my theory that the Phoenician Sailor represents the commerce of *lust* as well as the commerce of materialism."

10. *A Moment's Surrender: "What the Thunder Said"*

1. See Chapter 6, note 3, for citations of Grover Smith and Hugh Kenner studies.
2. *The Waste Land: A Facsimile*, p. 129.
3. For example, see Brooks, *"The Waste Land:* Critique of the Myth."
4. *The Waste Land: A Facsimile*, pp. 98–99.
5. Ibid., pp. 108–9.
6. Ibid., p. 129.
7. *The Autobiography of Bertrand Russell: 1914–1944*, p. 254.
8. Edwin Haviland Miller, ed. *A Century of Whitman Criticism* (Bloomington: Indiana University Press, 1969), pp. 162–63.
9. *The Waste Land: A Facsimile*, pp. 112–15.
10. Smith, *T.S. Eliot's Poetry and Plays*, p. 95.
11. *The Waste Land: A Facsimile*, p. 130.
12. *From Ritual to Romance*, pp. 175, 182.
13. Simpson, *Three on the Tower*, p. 146.
14. *The Brhadaranyaka Upanisad*, tr. Swami Madhavananda (Calcutta: Advaita Ashrama, 1965), pp. 813–17.
15. Knight, "Thoughts on *The Waste Land*," pp. 4–5.
16. Brooks, *"The Waste Land:* Critique of the Myth," p. 153; Williamson, *A Reader's Guide to T.S. Eliot*, p. 151; Smith, *T.S. Eliot's Poetry and Plays*, p. 96; Kenner, *The Invisible Poet*, p. 175.
17. Cecil Clementi, ed., *Pervigilium Veneris: The Vigil of Venus* (London: Henry Frowde, 1911), p. 35.
18. *Selected Writings of Gérard de Nerval*, tr. Geoffrey Wagner (Ann Arbor: University of Michigan Press, 1959), pp. 212–13. See also p. 252 for biographical background of the poem.
19. Quotations cited in the text are from Thomas Kyd, *The Spanish Tragedy* (London: Ernest Benn Limited, 1970).

11. *Funerals and Farewells: "Exequy" and "Elegy"*

1. *The Letters of Ezra Pound*, p. 169.
2. Ibid., p. 171.
3. Ibid., p. 169.
4. *The Waste Land: A Facsimile*, pp. 130–31.
5. "The Making of *The Waste Land*," p. 129.
6. *The Waste Land: A Facsimile*, pp. 118–21.
7. Ibid., pp. 100–101.
8. Ibid., p. 130.
9. Ibid., pp. 116–17.

12. *A Kind of Valediction: A Familiar Compound Ghost*

1. *To Criticize the Critic*, p. 128.
2. *Selected Essays* (1950), p. 8.
3. Ibid., pp. 208–9.

4. Graham Hough, "Dante and Eliot," *Critical Quarterly* 16, no. 4 (Winter 1974): 303.

5. *Word Unheard: A Guide through Eliot's Four Quartets* (London: Methuen, 1969), pp. 146–58.

6. Note George Watson's stress on the literary nature of the Eliot-Verdenal relationship in "Quest for a Frenchman," pp. 468–72.

13. Making The Waste Land *Mean*

1. Plimpton, *Writers at Work (Second Series)*, p. 105.

2. The fullest account of the relation of Eliot and Pound is to be found in Donald Gallup, *T.S. Eliot & Ezra Pound: Collaborators in Letters* (New Haven: Henry W. Wenning/ C.A. Stonehill, 1970). Although Gallup's reading of *The Waste Land* manuscripts is quite different from mine, his conclusion about Pound's understanding of the poem is quite close (p. 16): "Pound's major deletions in the central poem seem to reflect a lack of sympathy with some of the experiments that Eliot was trying to carry out. The poem which resulted from the Eliot-Pound collaboration was in some respects quite different from that which Eliot had had in mind. At least part of what the central poem gained in concentration, intensity, and general effectiveness through Pound's editing was at the sacrifice of some of its experimental character."

3. This and the following two quotes are found in Kenner, *The Invisibile Poet*, p. 152.

4. *The Letters of Ezra Pound*, pp. 180–81.

5. Quotations are from Edmund Wilson's essay, reprinted as "The Puritan Turned Artist," in *T.S. Eliot, The Waste Land: A Casebook*, pp. 100–101.

6. *The Use of Poetry and the Use of Criticism*, p. 13. Eliot was quoting and answering a footnote in I.A. Richards' *Science and Poetry* (1926). In the second edition of *Science and Poetry* (London: Kegan Paul, Trench, Trubner, 1935), pp. 70–71, Richards wrote: "The original footnote seems to have puzzled Mr. Eliot and some other readers. Well it might! In saying, though, that he 'had effected a complete severance between his poetry and all beliefs' I was referring not to the poet's own history, but to the technical detachment of the poetry. And the way in which he then seemed to have 'realized what otherwise have remained a speculative possibility' was by finding a new order through the contemplation and exhibition of disorder."

7. Quotes from I.A. Richards' comment on Eliot as reprinted in *T.S. Eliot, The Waste Land: A Casebook*, pp. 51, 53, 55.

8. F.R. Leavis, *New Bearings in English Poetry* (London: Chatto & Windus, 1950), p. 102.

9. "*The Waste Land:* Critique of the Myth," pp. 153, 156.

10. Ibid., pp. 160–61.

14. Letting The Waste Land *Be*

1. *The Use of Poetry and the Use of Criticism*, p. 151.

2. *On Poetry and Poets*, p. 107.

3. Ibid., p. 108.

Index